OECD/G20 Base Erosion and Profit Shifting Project

Developing a Multilateral Instrument to Modify Bilateral Tax Treaties, Action 15 -2015 Final Report

Please cite this publication as:
OECD (2015), *Developing a Multilateral Instrument to Modify Bilateral Tax Treaties, Action 15 -2015 Final Report*, OECD/G20 Base Erosion and Profit Shifting Project, OECD Publishing, Paris.
http://dx.doi.org/10.1787/9789264241688-en

ISBN 978-92-64-24167-1 (print)
ISBN 978-92-64-24168-8 (PDF)

Series: OECD/G20 Base Erosion and Profit Shifting Project
ISSN 2313-2604 (print)
ISSN 2313-2612 (online)

Photo credits: Cover © ninog – Fotolia.com

Corrigenda to OECD publications may be found on line at: *www.oecd.org/about/publishing/corrigenda.htm*.

Foreword

International tax issues have never been as high on the political agenda as they are today. The integration of national economies and markets has increased substantially in recent years, putting a strain on the international tax rules, which were designed more than a century ago. Weaknesses in the current rules create opportunities for base erosion and profit shifting (BEPS), requiring bold moves by policy makers to restore confidence in the system and ensure that profits are taxed where economic activities take place and value is created.

Following the release of the report *Addressing Base Erosion and Profit Shifting* in February 2013, OECD and G20 countries adopted a 15-point Action Plan to address BEPS in September 2013. The Action Plan identified 15 actions along three key pillars: introducing coherence in the domestic rules that affect cross-border activities, reinforcing substance requirements in the existing international standards, and improving transparency as well as certainty.

Since then, all G20 and OECD countries have worked on an equal footing and the European Commission also provided its views throughout the BEPS project. Developing countries have been engaged extensively via a number of different mechanisms, including direct participation in the Committee on Fiscal Affairs. In addition, regional tax organisations such as the African Tax Administration Forum, the *Centre de rencontre des administrations fiscales* and the *Centro Interamericano de Administraciones Tributarias*, joined international organisations such as the International Monetary Fund, the World Bank and the United Nations, in contributing to the work. Stakeholders have been consulted at length: in total, the BEPS project received more than 1 400 submissions from industry, advisers, NGOs and academics. Fourteen public consultations were held, streamed live on line, as were webcasts where the OECD Secretariat periodically updated the public and answered questions.

After two years of work, the 15 actions have now been completed. All the different outputs, including those delivered in an interim form in 2014, have been consolidated into a comprehensive package. The BEPS package of measures represents the first substantial renovation of the international tax rules in almost a century. Once the new measures become applicable, it is expected that profits will be reported where the economic activities that generate them are carried out and where value is created. BEPS planning strategies that rely on outdated rules or on poorly co-ordinated domestic measures will be rendered ineffective.

Implementation therefore becomes key at this stage. The BEPS package is designed to be implemented via changes in domestic law and practices, and via treaty provisions, with negotiations for a multilateral instrument under way and expected to be finalised in 2016. OECD and G20 countries have also agreed to continue to work together to ensure a consistent and co-ordinated implementation of the BEPS recommendations. Globalisation requires that global solutions and a global dialogue be established which go beyond OECD and G20 countries. To further this objective, in 2016 OECD and G20 countries will conceive an inclusive framework for monitoring, with all interested countries participating on an equal footing.

A better understanding of how the BEPS recommendations are implemented in practice could reduce misunderstandings and disputes between governments. Greater focus on implementation and tax administration should therefore be mutually beneficial to governments and business. Proposed improvements to data and analysis will help support ongoing evaluation of the quantitative impact of BEPS, as well as evaluating the impact of the countermeasures developed under the BEPS Project.

Table of contents

Abbreviations and acronyms

APA	Advance pricing agreement
BEPS	Base erosion and profit shifting
CFA	Committee on Fiscal Affairs
EU	European Union
ICAO	International Civil Aviation Organisation
ILO	International Labour Organisation
MAC	Convention on Mutual Administrative Assistance in Tax Matters
MAP	Mutual agreement procedure
OECD	Organisation for Economic Co-operation and Development
PE	Permanent establishment
SAARC	South Asian Association for Regional Cooperation
UN	United Nations
VCLT	Vienna Convention on the Law of Treaties

Executive summary

The endorsement of the *Action Plan on Base Erosion and Profit Shifting* (BEPS Action Plan, OECD, 2013) by the Leaders of the G20 in Saint-Petersburg in September 2013 shows unprecedented political support to adapt the current international tax system to the challenges of globalisation. Tax treaties are based on a set of common principles designed to eliminate double taxation that may occur in the case of cross-border trade and investments. The current network of bilateral tax treaties dates back to the 1920s and the first soft law Model Tax Convention developed by the League of Nations. The Organisation for Economic Co-operation and Development (OECD) and the United Nations (UN) have subsequently updated model tax conventions based on that work. The contents of those model tax conventions are reflected in thousands of bilateral agreements among jurisdictions.

Globalisation has exacerbated the impact of gaps and frictions among different countries' tax systems. As a result, some features of the current bilateral tax treaty system facilitate base erosion and profit shifting (BEPS) and need to be addressed. Beyond the challenges faced by the current tax treaty system on substance, the sheer number of bilateral treaties makes updating the current tax treaty network highly burdensome. Even where a change to the OECD Model Tax Convention is consensual, it takes a substantial amount of time and resources to introduce it into most bilateral tax treaties. As a result, the current network is not well-synchronised with the model tax conventions, and issues that arise over time cannot be addressed swiftly. Without a mechanism to swiftly implement them, changes to models only make the gap between the content of the models and the content of actual tax treaties wider. This clearly contradicts the political objective to strengthen the current system by putting an end to BEPS, in part by modifying the bilateral treaty network. Doing so is necessary not only to tackle BEPS, but also to ensure the sustainability of the consensual framework to eliminate double taxation. For this reason, governments have agreed to explore the feasibility of a multilateral instrument that would have the same effects as a simultaneous renegotiation of thousands of bilateral tax treaties.

Action 15 of the BEPS Action Plan provides for an analysis of the tax and public international law issues related to the development of a multilateral instrument to enable countries that wish to do so to implement measures developed in the course of the work on BEPS and amend bilateral tax treaties. On the basis of this analysis, interested countries will develop a multilateral instrument designed to provide an innovative approach to international tax matters, reflecting the rapidly evolving nature of the global economy and the need to adapt quickly to this evolution. The goal of Action 15 is to streamline the implementation of the tax treaty-related BEPS measures. This is an innovative approach with no exact precedent in the tax world, but precedents for modifying bilateral treaties with a multilateral instrument exist in various other areas of public international law. Drawing on the expertise of public international law and tax experts, the 2014 Report, which is reproduced hereafter, explored the technical feasibility of a multilateral hard law approach and its consequences on the current tax treaty system. It identified the issues arising from the development of such an instrument and provided an analysis of the international tax, public international law, and political issues that arise from such an approach.

The 2014 Report also concluded that a multilateral instrument is desirable and feasible, and that negotiations for such an instrument should be convened quickly. Based on this analysis, a mandate for the formation of an ad hoc Group ("the Group") to develop a multilateral instrument on tax treaty measures to tackle BEPS, which is reproduced hereafter, was approved by the OECD Committee on Fiscal Affairs and endorsed by the G20 Finance Ministers and Central Bank Governors in February 2015. The Group is open to participation from all interested countries on an equal footing and is served by the OECD Secretariat. The Group begun its work in May 2015 with the aim to conclude its work and open the multilateral instrument for signature by 31 December 2016. Participation in the development of the multilateral instrument is voluntary and does not entail any commitments to sign such instrument once it has been finalised.

A mandate for the development of a multilateral instrument on tax treaty measures to tackle BEPS

Preamble

Recognising that Action 15 of the *Action Plan on Base Erosion and Profit Shifting* (BEPS Action Plan, OECD, 2013) called for the development of a multilateral instrument to implement measures developed in the course of the work on BEPS and modify bilateral tax treaties;

Considering that the report *Developing a Multilateral Instrument to Modify Bilateral Tax Treaties* (OECD, 2014), which was approved by the Committee on Fiscal Affairs (CFA) and endorsed by the Leaders of the G20, concluded that a multilateral instrument is desirable and feasible, and that negotiations for such an instrument should be convened quickly;

Noting that the G20 Leaders Communiqué adopted in Brisbane on 16 November 2014 welcomes the significant progress of the BEPS Action Plan "to modernise international tax rules";

The countries participating in the OECD-G20 BEPS Project have agreed to establish an ad hoc Group (hereinafter "the Group") with the mandate set out below. They recognise that the Group is not a formal or informal OECD body and therefore participation of non-OECD members in the Group does not create, and cannot be interpreted to create, a precedent in the context of OECD procedures for the participation of non-members in OECD activities.

A. Objective

1. The Group shall develop a multilateral instrument to modify existing bilateral tax treaties solely in order to swiftly implement the tax treaty measures developed in the course of the OECD-G20 BEPS Project.

B. Participation

1. Membership of the Group is open to all interested States.
2. All members of the Group participate on an equal footing.
3. Non-State Jurisdictions can participate in the Group as Observers upon a specific invitation by the Group.
4. Relevant international and regional intergovernmental organisations can be invited by the Group to participate as Observers.

C. Duration

1. The Group will start its work no later than July 2015.
2. The Group will aim to conclude its work and open the multilateral instrument for signature by 31 December 2016.
3. The term of the mandate for the Group will end upon the opening of the multilateral instrument for signature.

D. Governance

1. The Plenary of the Group is the decision-making body of the Group.
2. The Plenary is assisted by:
   a. A Bureau appointed by the Plenary of the Group, which will prepare and guide the work of the Group; and
   b. Sub-groups or existing OECD bodies, as deemed appropriate by the Plenary.
3. The Plenary of the Group shall appoint a Chair and two Vice-Chairs at its first meeting, who are also Chair and Vice Chairs of the Bureau.
4. The Group is convened under the aegis of the OECD and G20 and is served by the OECD Secretariat.
5. The functioning of the Group and its sub-groups will be governed by the OECD Rules of Procedure and the provisions of international law related to the development and conclusion of treaties.
6. The Group will provide periodic updates to the CFA regarding progress made and will consult with the Committee and its subsidiary bodies as necessary and appropriate.

E. Funding

1. The functioning of the Group will be funded by its members.
2. Members and Observers in the Group will be responsible for covering the costs of their participation in the work of the Group.

2014 Report – Developing a Multilateral Instrument to Modify Bilateral Tax Treaties

Introduction

1. **There is strong political support to eliminate BEPS.** In an environment of severe fiscal consolidation and social hardship, BEPS has become a high priority for governments. BEPS relates chiefly to instances where the interaction of different tax rules leads to double non-taxation or less than single taxation. It also relates to arrangements that achieve no or low taxation by shifting profits away from the jurisdictions where those profits are generated. The OECD/G20 BEPS Project aims to address BEPS concerns in a comprehensive manner.

2. **The current system of bilateral tax treaties focuses on the elimination of double taxation.** The interaction of domestic tax systems can lead to overlaps in the exercise of taxing rights that can result in double taxation. For example, if an item of income is earned in one jurisdiction (the "source jurisdiction") by a resident of another jurisdiction (the "residence jurisdiction"), both jurisdictions may tax that income under their domestic laws. International treaties to address double taxation, many of which originated with principles developed by the League of Nations in the 1920s, aim to address these overlaps so as to minimise trade distortions and impediments to sustainable economic growth. The resulting network of more than 3000 bilateral tax treaties, based on model tax conventions, is very valuable. It ensures that there is broad consistency in the tax rules applicable to cross-border trade and investment. Countries around the world agree on the need to eliminate double taxation and to do so on the basis of agreed international rules that are clear and predictable, giving certainty to both businesses and governments.

3. **However, some features of the current tax treaty system facilitate BEPS.** The interrelationship between domestic tax laws and the international tax framework is a key pillar in supporting the growth of the global economy. However, as globalisation has changed the way business is done, the gaps and frictions that were always present in the existing bilateral tax treaties have grown more important. Existing tax treaty provisions are sometimes exploited, in some cases in conjunction with domestic law rules, so that large amounts of income are not subject to tax in any jurisdiction. Moreover, the existing bilateral tax treaties vary widely in their details, including when the differences are not necessary to reflect specificities in the economic relations between the two contracting states. Rather, certain differences in detail appear to be due to the fact that treaties have been negotiated over a long period of time, and in some circumstances these differences create opportunities for BEPS, which are then exploited by taxpayers.

4. **Change is needed to eliminate the opportunities the current tax treaty system creates for double non-taxation.** The BEPS Action Plan identifies treaty abuse as one of the most important sources of BEPS concerns. OECD and non-OECD government tax treaty experts agree that changes to the model tax conventions, as well as the bilateral tax treaties based on those model conventions, are required to stop or significantly reduce these abuses. A wide range of specific issues addressed in current model tax conventions, including changes to the definition of permanent establishment (PE), and improvements to dispute resolution procedures are being considered by leading tax treaty negotiators from

OECD and G20 governments. These tax treaty experts have also identified the need for new model treaty provisions targeted at specific issues that generally were not addressed in bilateral tax treaties, including the introduction of an anti-treaty abuse provision in relation to hybrid mismatch arrangements, and the compatibility with tax treaties of certain anti-BEPS measures. The work is expected to be finalised in 2015.

5. **The sheer number of bilateral treaties makes updates to the treaty network burdensome and time-consuming, limiting the efficiency of multilateral efforts.** After any change to the model tax conventions is agreed multilaterally, it takes a substantial amount of time and resources to introduce that change into most bilateral tax treaties. Indeed, renegotiating a country's treaty network takes decades. As a result, the current network is not well-synchronised with the model tax conventions. Since the actual treaties are many years behind the models on which they are based, any multilaterally-agreed changes to the models take a generation to implement.

6. **In contrast the need for change is urgent, and this is both a challenge and a unique opportunity.** The BEPS Action Plan was developed quickly because of political imperatives to address BEPS, and the expectation is that agreement on how to solve the problem will be implemented quickly as well. However, multilaterally-agreed changes to the model tax conventions to tackle BEPS only make the gap between the content of the model tax conventions and the content of actual tax treaties wider. To address BEPS in a reasonable timeframe, a mechanism to facilitate swifter implementation is hence required. This is challenging but at the same time creates a unique opportunity to modernise the architecture of the international tax treaty network.

7. **A multilateral instrument can address treaty-based BEPS issues while respecting sovereign autonomy in tax matters.** The concept of sovereign autonomy is a basic principle underpinning the international order and providing the foundation for the negotiation of international treaties. In tax matters, the concept of sovereignty underpins the stable tax framework within which governments have been able to facilitate arrangements that allowed for the benefits of globalisation to flow to all market economies. Governments have historically used domestic legislation and bilateral treaties to reach the appropriate balance between national sovereignty and international co-operation in this area. As BEPS results from the interactions of multiple countries' laws and treaties, governments need to collaborate more intensively through a hard law multilateral instrument both to prevent the tax treaty network from facilitating BEPS and to protect their tax sovereignty. Recognising the tax sovereignty concern, the report focuses on implementing treaty measures, even though a multilateral instrument could in principle also be used to express commitments to implement certain domestic law measures.

8. **A multilateral instrument facilitates speedy action and innovation.** A multilateral instrument will implement agreed treaty measures over a reasonably short period and at the same time it would preserve the bilateral nature of tax treaties. This innovative approach has at least three important advantages. First, it would help ensure that the multilateral instrument is highly targeted. Second, it would allow all existing bilateral tax treaties to be modified in a synchronised way with respect to BEPS issues, without a need to individually address each treaty within the 3000+ treaty network. Third, it responds to the political imperatives driving the BEPS Project: it allows BEPS abuses to be curtailed and governments to swiftly achieve their international tax policy goals without creating the risk of violating existing bilateral treaties that would derive from the use of unilateral and uncoordinated measures.

9. **Overcoming traditional obstacles to swiftly implement agreed tax treaty measures requires political willingness to act.** The efficiency and innovation represented by a targeted multilateral instrument does come with certain challenges. First, bilateral treaties are highly varied in their details, and there are limited precedents for modifying bilateral treaties with a multilateral instrument. Technical challenges therefore must be given careful attention. Second, even when solutions to the technical issues are available, the trade-offs in terms of respecting sovereign rights, providing consistency, and achieving political acceptance from a critical mass of jurisdictions requires strong impetus at the highest political level. Meeting these challenges is necessary not only to tackle BEPS, but also to strengthen and ensure the future sustainability of the existing consensual framework to eliminate double taxation. With political will, however, even difficult treaty-based challenges can be met successfully and swiftly. The recent work on the *Convention on Mutual Administrative Assistance in Tax Matters* (hereafter "MAC"), which was undertaken at the direction of the G20 in connection with Leaders' desire to address offshore tax evasion, provides one example of the impact G20 leadership can have in the international tax area.

10. **This report concludes that a multilateral instrument is desirable and feasible, and that negotiations should be convened quickly.** The present report explores the questions raised by the use of a targeted multilateral instrument to modify tax treaties, and provides a high-level analysis of both the technical (public international law and international tax law) and political issues that arise. It highlights the feasibility of a multilateral approach as the way to streamline the implementation of the BEPS Action Plan with a view to responding to the current state of urgency, and also to improve efficiency. It concludes that a multilateral instrument is desirable and feasible and it should be negotiated through an International Conference open to G20 countries, OECD members and other interested countries and convened under the aegis of the OECD and the G20. The mandate of the Conference should be limited in scope (implementing the BEPS Action Plan) and in time (no more than 2 years). The Conference could also be invited to reflect on possible further steps to continue to streamline the implementation of agreed changes to the existing model tax conventions and could make recommendations in that respect.

A recent success story: the Convention on Mutual Administrative Assistance in Tax Matters

The *Convention on Mutual Administrative Assistance in Tax Matters* ("Convention") was opened for signature by the member states of the Council of Europe and the OECD in 1988, entered into force in 1995, and had only 14 signatories as of 2009. At its April 2009 London Summit the G20 Leaders called on the OECD to modernise this instrument to align it to contemporary international standards on exchange of information, and to open it to all countries, by stating in the *G20 Declaration on Strengthening the Financial System* that they were "*committed to developing proposals, by end 2009, to make it easier for developing countries to secure the benefits of a new cooperative tax environment*" (G20, 2009). A Protocol to the Convention was negotiated in 2009 and the amended Convention was presented at the annual OECD Ministerial meeting in May 2010, and the amended Convention and Protocol were opened for signature by a wide range of countries on 1st June 2011. As of 3 July 2014, 66 countries, including all G20 countries, had signed the amended Convention, and 14 jurisdictions were covered by territorial extension. The Convention – a single multilateral legal instrument – performs functions that would have otherwise required negotiating over 1800 new bilateral agreements. By means of the Convention, the G20 swiftly and successfully initiated a step change in transparency in cross-border tax matters globally.

1. A multilateral instrument is desirable and feasible

A. Developing a multilateral instrument is desirable: The benefits are numerous, while burdens can be addressed or avoided

11. **Changes to the OECD Model Tax Convention are intended to ultimately produce changes to the network of bilateral tax treaties that form a key component of the broader international tax architecture.** G20 Leaders endorsed the BEPS Action Plan, and committed to take the necessary individual and collective actions in order to tackle BEPS. The 15 BEPS Action Plan deliverables span three different areas: recommendations for domestic law taking the form of best practices and model domestic rules, other reports, as well as changes to the OECD Model Tax Convention and internationally agreed guidance on implementation. Tax treaty-related issues are agreed to be a key focus of BEPS concerns. The development of a multilateral instrument to tackle these treaty-based BEPS issues first of all requires agreement on the substance of the tax treaty measures required to respond to BEPS. Working groups are making steady and important progress towards this goal. Indeed, the first outputs are being made public at the same time as this report, while other outputs are expected by 2015.

12. **A multilateral negotiation can overcome the hurdle of cumbersome bilateral negotiations and produce important efficiency gains.** Given the decades-long process for bilateral treaty negotiations, a multilateral instrument represents the only way to address treaty-based BEPS concerns in a swift and co-ordinated manner. The current network of bilateral treaties involves substantial complexity because each treaty is a legally distinct instrument, and its relationship to other bilateral treaties is undefined. As a result, lawyers, tax administrators, and courts spend a lot of energy interpreting each individual treaty, especially when treaties differ in small ways. This problem would become more severe if varied anti-BEPS measures were included in thousands of new bilateral protocols to existing treaties. The multilateral instrument will instead produce synchronised results that would save resources and improve the clarity of BEPS-related international tax treaty rules. These benefits are in addition to the simple reality that only a multilateral instrument can overcome the practical difficulties associated with trying to rapidly modify the 3000+ bilateral treaty network.

13. **The multilateral instrument can provide developing countries with the opportunity to fully benefit from the BEPS Project.** For developing countries, the practical problems that are encountered in trying to address BEPS from within the bilateral tax treaty system alone are even more relevant than for developed countries. Developing countries find it more difficult than other countries both to conclude double tax treaties, and to interest other countries in tax treaty (re)negotiation, and their tax treaty negotiation expertise is often more limited than in the governments of developed economies. A multilateral instrument therefore offers the best opportunity to ensure that developing countries reap the benefits of multilateral efforts to tackle BEPS. In a multilateral negotiation, similarly-minded developing

governments may co-operate, pooling their expertise to be efficacious in the negotiating process.

14. **Some issues are much easier to address multilaterally than in bilateral instruments.** The bilateral treaty architecture was not originally designed to address high levels of factor mobility and global value chains. For example, globalisation substantially increases the need to resolve multi-country tax disputes. Although competent authorities within tax administrations have expressed interest in the possibility of developing a multilateral mutual agreement procedure (MAP) to resolve such multi-country disputes, some countries foresee legal constraints in the absence of a hard law instrument authorising multilateral MAP. Other countries do not believe they can use MAP to resolve cases that touch on issues not explicitly addressed in their existing bilateral tax treaties in the absence of an international law instrument that provides that authority. These and other legal obstacles that arise in implementing multilateral MAP can easily be addressed in the context of the multilateral instrument.

15. **A multilateral instrument can increase the consistency and help ensure the continued reliability of the international tax treaty network, providing additional certainty for business.** In contrast to amendments to thousands of bilateral tax treaties, a targeted multilateral instrument to address BEPS would be much more likely to produce consistent results. The multilateral nature of the instrument would focus the attention of a large number of highly qualified treaty negotiators on a single document that could incorporate the language deemed most appropriate by all concerned countries. In addition, having a single text, instead of thousands of similar but slightly varying texts, would be more likely to produce consistent interpretation across jurisdictional boundaries. As a result, a common international understanding would develop about the meaning of the text of the provisions of the multilateral instrument. By addressing a number of contested questions surrounding international tax rules in a definitive way, a multilateral instrument can restore clarity and ensure future certainty for the status of a variety of important rules that business relies upon to be able to invest with confidence cross-border.

16. **Flexibility, respect for bilateral relations, and a targeted scope are key to success.** The benefits of swift implementation, improved consistency, certainty, and efficiency, can only be achieved if bilateral specificities and tax sovereignty are fully respected, so that the process does not bog down or involve too few countries. Allowing countries to tailor their commitment under the instrument in pre-defined cases can help address these concerns. On the other hand, in order to feel comfortable moving ahead in tackling BEPS, countries will want assurance that other countries are tackling BEPS simultaneously. Parties could therefore commit to a core set of provisions as part of a multilateral instrument, but then have the possibility to opt-out, opt-in or choose between alternative – and clearly delineated – provisions with respect to other issues covered by the instrument. Negotiations would thereby accommodate bilateral specificities, reinforce governmental policy goals, and reassert tax sovereignty in the face of globalisation.

17. **At the same time, a level playing field will require broad participation.** Some provisions of the treaty-based portion of the BEPS Project require broad participation in order to successfully address BEPS concerns. Thus, to ensure a level playing field and fairly shared tax burdens, flexibility and respect for bilateral relations will need to be balanced against core commitments that reflect new international standards that countries are urged to meet and for which the multilateral instrument is a facilitative tool.

B. Developing a multilateral instrument is feasible: Legal mechanisms are available to achieve a balanced instrument that addresses the technical and political challenges

18. **The technical legal challenges that arise in modifying the international tax treaty architecture by means of a multilateral instrument will require careful attention.** Nevertheless, an analysis of precedents in other areas of international law and the specifics of various proposed changes to the model tax conventions illustrate that developing a multilateral instrument to rapidly implement agreed changes is completely feasible from a legal point of view.

19. **The multilateral instrument would coexist with the existing bilateral tax treaty network.** The most promising approach for pursuing the goal of a multilateral instrument to consistently modify the existing, varied, 3000+ tax treaty architecture involves developing a multilateral instrument that would co-exist with bilateral tax treaties. Like existing tax treaties, this instrument would be governed by international law and would be legally binding on the parties. A multilateral instrument will modify a limited number of provisions common to most existing bilateral treaties, and would, for those treaties that do not already have such provisions, add new provisions specifically designed to counter BEPS. It could also clarify the compatibility with tax treaties of other anti-BEPS measures developed in the course of the BEPS Project. The multilateral instrument could be accompanied by an explanatory report to facilitate the implementation of the provisions contained therein.

20. **This approach will ensure that the multilateral instrument is highly targeted and efficient.** A multilateral instrument that coexists with bilateral tax treaties was identified to be more appropriate than other approaches because it is more efficient and more targeted. Other options that were evaluated included (1) the use of a "self-standing instrument" that would wholly supersede bilateral tax treaties, governing the relationship between all the parties, whether or not they have concluded bilateral tax treaties amongst themselves and (2) an instrument whose sole purpose would be to operate like a bundle of "amending protocols", precisely amending the varying language of each of the 3000+ tax treaties. A "self-standing instrument" that would wholly supersede bilateral tax treaties was viewed to be overbroad given the importance of bilateral relations in international tax affairs and the importance of preserving tax sovereignty. A bundle of "amending protocols" was viewed as less appealing than a coexisting multilateral instrument because it would be both more technically complex and less efficient. As a result, this approach was viewed as being too cumbersome and time consuming to satisfy the central purpose of the multilateral instrument, which is to implement treaty-related responses to BEPS quickly.

21. **A multilateral instrument would follow established negotiating processes, and ratification would require conventional domestic procedures, pursuant to national laws.** The intent of this multilateral instrument would be to ensure the effective and efficient implementation of the outputs of the BEPS Project that bear a relationship to the operation of tax treaties. Once the implications of this innovative solution have been fully considered and addressed, an International Conference would negotiate the content and actual text of the multilateral instrument, which would then be subject to the regular ratification procedures by each party. Therefore, this multilateral instrument would follow traditional negotiating processes, and ratification would take place according to national laws.

22. **The relationship between parties to a multilateral instrument that are not parties to a bilateral tax treaty between themselves generally would not be affected.** In some instances, parties to a multilateral instrument will not yet have concluded a bilateral tax treaty between themselves. In general, a multilateral instrument would only govern the

relationship between parties that have concluded bilateral tax treaties amongst themselves. One exception to this general rule could be a multilateral dispute resolution mechanism which operates among all parties to the multilateral instrument, including in cases where certain parties to the instrument lack bilateral treaty relationships with one another.[1] A separate question to be examined by the treaty negotiators at the International Conference is whether this multilateral instrument would impose any obligation on the parties to the instrument with respect to a situation in which two States conclude a bilateral tax treaty covering the same issue for the first time at a date after they each become parties to the instrument. From a legal point of view the relevant provisions could be crafted to apply in such a case, and therefore a decision will have to be taken at the political level.

23. **Technical challenges arising from the interaction between a multilateral instrument and bilateral tax treaties can be addressed.**

- **Variations in scope between similar provisions of existing bilateral treaties can be successfully resolved.** The prospective treaty outputs of the BEPS Project will take into account current best practices in tax treaty negotiation and therefore the provisions of a multilateral instrument could, to a certain extent, overlap with certain provisions found in some bilateral tax treaties. Potential conflicts may arise from the interaction between new multilaterally agreed provisions and similar provisions included in some existing bilateral treaties that fully or partly cover the same subject matter. Such cases raise questions as to whether existing bilateral provisions incorporated in existing tax treaties should remain fully or partially applicable alongside a multilaterally-agreed provision designed to address the same basic questions, and if so under what circumstances and to what extent. From a legal standpoint, the interaction between multilaterally agreed provisions and similar provisions of existing bilateral treaties could be resolved through the inclusion of specific "compatibility" clauses (or "primacy" clauses) in the multilateral instrument.
- **Variations in the wording of similar provisions of existing bilateral treaties can be addressed through superseding language in a multilateral instrument.** Introducing multilaterally agreed changes through a multilateral instrument may raise technical challenges due to variations in the wording of existing bilateral tax treaties. Whether this is a real issue will depend largely on the extent to which each treaty-based output of the BEPS Project is a stand-alone measure which easily complements existing treaties, or relies heavily on existing concepts that are already defined in model tax conventions. If a given output of the BEPS Project relies on an existing concept, and those concepts do not appear, or have an alternative meaning, in some bilateral treaties, a multilateral instrument will be unable to assume uniform usage of the Model Tax Convention concept. However, negotiators of a multilateral instrument can address this issue by ensuring that the instrument defines its own terms when necessary, and does so in a way that is compatible with the range of existing bilateral treaties. Similarly, specifying the provision of existing bilateral treaties that is being addressed in a multilateral instrument through general description rather than specific textual cross-references can ensure that minor differences in the wording of existing tax treaty provisions do not pose an obstacle for uniform effect and implementation of an agreed provision in a multilateral instrument. The explanatory report to this multilateral instrument can give examples and further ensure consistency of understanding regarding the interaction of a multilateral instrument and existing bilateral tax treaties.

- **Addressing variations in the numbering of provisions simply requires careful drafting.** Multilaterally agreed measures being developed in the course of the BEPS Project will likely use numerical cross-references to existing provisions of the model conventions as a shorthand to give technical precision to the treaty-based proposals to address BEPS. However, the numerical cross-references in most treaties do not align precisely with the numbering of the model conventions. As a result, model bilateral treaty provision cross-references cannot be transposed directly into a multilateral instrument. In principle, this potential issue can be addressed by a multilateral instrument that avoids explicit numerical cross-references to articles of the model tax conventions or specific articles of existing bilateral treaties, and instead clearly cross-references the relevant subject matter of bilateral treaties with appropriate language. Practical issues associated with this approach are likely to be identified and resolved in the context of negotiation of the multilateral instrument.
- **The timelines for signature and entry into force can be calibrated for flexibility.** In particular, it would be possible to set up different dates for the entry into force of the instrument for the parties depending on the provisions of the instrument (e.g. some provisions could enter into force at the start of a new tax year while other could enter into force at the date of ratification). In addition, express mechanisms and procedures could be incorporated into a multilateral instrument to ensure expeditious amendment procedures in the future. These mechanisms would be consistent with traditional negotiating processes, and ratification would require conventional domestic procedures.
- **Solutions for other technical issues, such as questions of language and translation, are readily available.** Language issues may arise with respect to the modification of bilateral tax treaties authenticated in languages different from the authenticated language(s) of the multilateral instrument. Drafting a multilateral instrument in a number of languages would increase its cost, the risk of conflict between versions in different languages and practical challenges in its administration. This question has arisen in other areas of international law, and precedents support various potential solutions.

24. **In general, a flexible approach will be paramount for the multilateral instrument.** As is reflected in the existing network of bilateral tax treaties, parties to a multilateral instrument may have tax policies that differ from one another and could not be harmonised amongst all the parties to the instrument. They may not be ready to accept the same precise commitments vis-à-vis all other parties. One of the main challenges for negotiators of a multilateral instrument will therefore be to ensure flexibility regarding the extent of the rights and obligations established by the treaty vis-à-vis all the other parties, as well as the level of commitments towards certain parties, while at the same time maintaining consistency, in order to create a level playing field, and transparency, in order to provide certainty.

25. **There are ample legal means for providing flexibility to modulate, within agreed boundaries, parties' commitments.** It is possible for a multilateral instrument to allow for the tailoring of the level of certain commitments towards all the other parties and/or depending on the partner country. There are a number of tools to ensure flexibility and a number of relevant precedents in this regard. It should be recognised that some provisions may require consistent adoption among the parties to a multilateral instrument for reasons of technical administrability.

26. **The relationship with other multilateral instruments should be closely examined.** Once the work on the actual measures is completed, the relationship of a multilateral instrument with European Union (EU) law and other relevant multilateral agreements, e.g. regional tax treaties such as the Nordic tax treaty, will also need to be addressed.

27. **Negotiation of the multilateral instrument must be speedy to avoid uncertainty.** It is quite important for measures countering BEPS to be agreed and put in place quickly, so that business may adjust to the new reality and continue to support growth, create jobs, and foster innovation. At the same time, it is worth underlining that putting some issues within a multilateral instrument could in principle slow the ability to address BEPS, by extending the timetable for responding to other parts of the BEPS agenda. In this context, a targeted multilateral instrument with a well-defined scope and a precise timetable for negotiation is key.

28. **The BEPS Project is intended to result in shared principles to shore up the clarity and predictability of the tax treatment of cross-border activities.** Once bilateral tax treaties are modified through a multilateral instrument, it will be important to ensure clarity so that the interaction between the multilateral instrument and bilateral tax treaties is clearly outlined. One of the challenges related to the development of a flexible multilateral instrument involves ensuring that mechanisms and procedures are developed and put in place to achieve full transparency. From a legal standpoint, a number of mechanisms are available, such as the publication of versions of bilateral tax treaties that also include the relevant provisions of the multilateral instrument, a system of notifications deposited by pairs of parties for permitted opt-outs or opt-ins, etc.

29. **Mechanisms to resolve the technical challenges that might arise from the use of a multilateral instrument, and relevant precedents in other areas of international law, are described in more detail in the annex to this report**. An informal group of eminent experts in tax and public international law was gathered in September 2013 to work with the OECD Secretariat on an analysis of the issues arising from the development of a multilateral instrument. The Secretariat developed the technical annex to this report *A toolbox for a multilateral instrument for the swift implementation of BEPS measures* based on input received from these experts. It provides illustrative solutions to potential issues lying at the interstices of international tax law and public international law and how they could be successfully addressed by a multilateral instrument.

Note

1. In the absence of bilateral treaty relationships between all of the parties, a number of governments are of the view that a multilateral MAP or advance pricing agreement (APA) would only be possible where the multilateral instrument itself contains a specific multilateral MAP provision as well as an exchange of information provision that would permit taxpayer information to be exchanged between all the parties (assuming there is not some other basis for exchange of information between the parties, such as the MAC or a bilateral Tax Information Exchange Agreement).

2. The nature of the treaty-related BEPS measures will facilitate the conclusion of a targeted multilateral instrument, which could be further expanded at a later date

30. **The multilateral instrument provides an innovative approach to address the rapidly evolving nature of the global economy and the need to adapt international rules quickly.** Changes to the OECD Model Tax Convention are intended to produce changes to the network of bilateral tax treaties that forms a key component of the broader international tax architecture. This is, for example, the case for the introduction of an anti-treaty abuse provision, changes to the definition of PE, improvements to dispute resolution procedures, and the introduction of treaty provisions in relation to hybrid mismatch arrangements. It may also include provisions that clarify the relationship with double tax treaties of special measures that aim to counter abuses. As outlined above, the main objective of a multilateral instrument would be to modify existing bilateral tax treaties, in a synchronised and efficient manner, to implement treaty measures developed in the course of the BEPS Project, without a need to individually renegotiate each treaty within the 3000+ treaty network.

31. **Some of the measures developed in the BEPS Project are multilateral in nature.** A number of treaty-based outputs of the BEPS Project can be drafted as stand-alone measures that complement and co-exist with bilateral tax treaties. These provisions can be directly implemented without the need to take bilateral specificities into account. Indeed, some provisions would be much more effective if implemented through a multilateral instrument. The paragraphs below note a few potential provisions that are multilateral in nature and which could be introduced by a multilateral instrument.

- **Multilateral MAP:** as highlighted above in section 1 of this report, there is merit in developing a truly multilateral MAP if the goal is to resolve multi-country disputes. Such a provision would enable MAP consultation with the competent authority of all parties to a multilateral instrument that are concerned with a case involving a taxpayer active in many jurisdictions. To provide certainty and resolution of disputes in the post-BEPS environment, such a provision would further provide for arbitration where the competent authorities are unable to resolve the case by mutual agreement.
- **Addressing dual-residence structures:** although dual-residence for business entities is relatively rare, an increasing number of BEPS strategies involve dual-resident companies. Given the risk of abuse arising from the use of these structures, countries may conclude that it is better to address dual-residence situations on a case-by-case basis in order to deter aggressive tax planning that facilitates BEPS. However, this simple anti-abuse measure would be most effective if adopted consistently across the existing bilateral tax treaty network.
- **Addressing transparent entities in the context of hybrid mismatch arrangements**: hybrid mismatch arrangements often lead to "double non-taxation" that may not be

intended by either country, or to unintended long-term tax deferral. It is difficult to determine unequivocally which individual country has lost tax revenue under such arrangements, but they often impact negatively on tax revenues, and also undermine transparency and fairness. Addressing hybrid mismatch arrangements comprehensively requires changes to domestic law. Nevertheless, a coherent policy response that also avoids double taxation would be facilitated – both at the domestic level and at the multilateral level – by consistently modifying existing tax treaties so that the eligibility for tax treaty benefits of payments made to entities in another jurisdiction is determined based on whether the payment is considered to be income of a resident for purposes of the tax law of the jurisdiction of residence of the payee.

- **Addressing "triangular" cases involving PEs in third states:** so-called triangular cases can arise where income of a tax treaty resident is attributed by the country of residence to a PE in a third State and exempt from tax in the residence State, often together with low taxation in the State of the PE. Bilateral treaties can provide rules that partially address such cases, but comprehensively addressing the problem requires incorporating a solution into all of a country's tax treaties. Thus, a multilateral instrument represents the most efficient mechanism for action.
- **Addressing treaty abuse:** there are a number of arrangements through which a person who is not a resident of a treaty country may inappropriately obtain the tax benefits that a bilateral tax treaty is intended to provide on a reciprocal basis to appropriate claimants. A multilateral instrument could incorporate approaches to prevent the granting of treaty benefits in inappropriate circumstances.

32. **Some tax treaty provisions that may implicate BEPS concerns are bilateral in nature, and for these provisions flexibility can be provided within certain boundaries.** Some treaty outputs of the BEPS Project may need to reflect specificities in the economic relations and/or in existing bilateral tax treaties between pairs of parties. For instance, a multilaterally agreed provision which introduces changes to the definition of PE may need to provide for some flexibility to tailor the level of commitment towards all the other parties and/or depending on the partner country. At the same time, flexibility has to be within certain boundaries to ensure consistency and administrative feasibility. Generally, it will be important to determine a set of core provisions to which all parties to a multilateral instrument will have to adhere to ensure a consistent and internally coherent approach to addressing treaty-related BEPS issues.

33. **The precise content of a multilateral instrument is yet to be defined but the sense of direction is clear.** OECD and G20 governments are vigorously working towards agreement on substantive treaty-based measures to counter BEPS. Although the final outputs in all areas are not expected until 2015, discussions indicate the need for substantial changes to model treaties and a corollary desire to speedily implement those changes into bilateral tax treaties. Indeed, other reports made available to the G20 at the same time as this report already provide substantive recommendations for change in a number of treaty-based areas. A multilateral instrument might also facilitate coordination across a wider range of BEPS-related issues. For example, the implementation of work on country-by-country reporting may be facilitated by the use of a multilateral instrument which also includes rules regarding the confidentiality of the information obtained by tax administrations. Similarly, problems of both double taxation and double-non-taxation associated with expense allocation are particularly noteworthy in the context of interest expense. A multilateral interest expense allocation agreement could be implemented through the multilateral instrument. It also may

be possible to develop new dispute resolution mechanisms that could further ensure that double taxation does not result from unilateral and uncoordinated responses to BEPS.

34. **A multilateral instrument to implement BEPS outputs is an effective and innovative solution.** This feasibility study concludes that despite potential challenges, a multilateral instrument is a promising way to quickly implement treaty-related BEPS measures. The G20 asked for this feasibility study to be prepared in parallel to the development of the actual measures to counter BEPS-related issues so as to most efficiently lay the groundwork for implementation. Continuing that process would require convening an International Conference to implement treaty-related BEPS measures. The mandate of the Conference should be limited in time and in scope (implementing the BEPS Action Plan).

35. **A multilateral instrument should be conceived in a dynamic way.** Many countries recognise the need to update their international tax rules to reflect changed circumstances of international business, and tax treaties are an important part of that process. Recognising that the initial work is focused on BEPS-related treaty measures, it is sensible to also reflect on possible further steps to continue to streamline the implementation of changes to the international tax treaty architecture using the same mechanism. For example, further updates to the model tax conventions might be implemented multilaterally. On the other hand, any decision to address a broader range of international tax issues multilaterally would represent a more significant step towards multilateralism in tax matters than the current work to use a multilateral instrument to address BEPS-related tax treaty issues. For the moment, it is important to keep the multilateral instrument narrowly targeted, and at the same time start a reflection on what further incremental opportunities may be available.

3. Next steps: Scoping the International Conference

36. **The treaty-based BEPS actions must be completed before the substantive components of the multilateral instrument can be finalised.** The development of a multilateral instrument requires framework provisions related to its entry into force, language, etc. and more importantly agreement on the substance of the tax treaty measures required to respond to BEPS. The OECD/G20 BEPS Project is making steady progress towards the development of those measures. Some of the treaty-based BEPS outputs will be delivered by September 2014, while a number of others will be delivered in 2015. Plans for an International Conference to negotiate a multilateral instrument that implements agreed treaty-based measures to tackle BEPS must take this timetable into account.

37. **This report recommends convening an International Conference to develop the multilateral instrument in 2015.** In accordance with standard treaty-making practice, an International Conference should be convened to develop the multilateral instrument. The International Conference should be open to all interested countries, under the aegis of the OECD and the G20. To maintain momentum, the work on the framework provisions of the multilateral instrument should begin in 2015. Once the recommendations for BEPS-related treaty measures are finalised in the context of the BEPS Project, they can then be considered by the International Conference and included in the multilateral instrument. In addition to incorporating the BEPS-related treaty measures, the International Conference should reflect on whether further protocols or similar multilateral instruments could be used in the future to foster a more effective international tax environment.

38. **On that basis it is recommended that, if the present proposal is endorsed, a mandate be quickly developed so that the International Conference be gathered in early 2015 to start its work.**

Annex A

A toolbox for a multilateral instrument for the swift implementation of BEPS measures

Executive summary

1. This annex offers a toolbox of theoretical options which could be used, as appropriate, in the development of a multilateral instrument for the swift implementation of base erosion and profit shifting (BEPS) measures. The options presented are based on an analysis of doctrine and precedents in public international law. It draws on the work of the informal group of experts on the multilateral instrument, a group comprised of both experts in public international law and experts in international taxation set up by the Committee on Fiscal Affairs (CFA) to advise on the feasibility of a multilateral instrument. The annex is structured around the three key conclusions: a multilateral instrument can (1) implement BEPS measures and modify the existing network of bilateral tax treaties; (2) provide appropriate flexibility in their level of commitment; and (3) ensure transparency and clarity for all stakeholders.

2. (1) The objective of the multilateral instrument would be the implementation of measures to address BEPS and its consequence would be the modification of certain provisions of the existing network of bilateral tax treaties. The bilateral tax treaties would remain in force for all non-BEPS related issues. It would be preferable, for reasons of efficiency and transparency, to define this relationship through the inclusion of compatibility clauses in the multilateral instrument. There are several options in order to ensure consistency in the interpretation and implementation of the multilateral instrument. Solutions also exist with regard to the dates of entry into force of different provisions and logistical issues including differences in the authentic languages of the multilateral instrument and bilateral tax treaties.

3. (2) As appropriate, the multilateral instrument can offer parties flexibility in their level of commitment within certain defined boundaries in order to move towards a level playing field. Defined flexibility as to the level of commitment of the parties vis-à-vis all or certain parties can be achieved through the use of opt-out mechanisms allowing parties to exclude or modify the legal effects of certain provisions; a choice between alternative – and clearly delineated – provisions; and opt-in mechanisms offering parties the possibility to take on additional commitments. The level of commitment of parties can also be modulated through the language used in the multilateral instrument (strong or soft wording) and types of obligations (of results and/or means).

4. (3) Considering the complexity of the network of bilateral tax treaties and the number of interested stakeholders (tax administrations, tax payers, third parties), it is vital that the multilateral instrument ensures the transparency and clarity of the commitments undertaken by the parties. Mechanisms are available to ensure clear and publicly accessible

information as regards, on the one hand, the interaction between the multilateral instrument and bilateral tax treaties and, on the other hand, the use of the mechanisms for flexibility set up by the multilateral instrument.

5. The annex concludes that a multilateral instrument to implement the measures developed in the course of the work on BEPS is feasible and would be the most efficient way to modify the existing network of bilateral tax treaties. A multilateral instrument offers an expansive and adaptable toolkit: once the substantive measures have been agreed, all the necessary mechanisms exist to reflect them as multilateral undertakings. As with the development of any new instrument, there are technical issues but they can be solved through well-tested solutions drawing on treaty law and practice. International tax experts and public international law experts will need to continue working hand in hand as this project moves forward.

Introduction

6. Action 15 of the BEPS Action Plan mandates the analysis of tax and public international law issues related to the development of a multilateral instrument to enable interested parties to implement measures developed in the course of the work on BEPS and amend bilateral tax treaties. Action 15 refers to a "multilateral instrument" i.e. a treaty concluded between more than two parties. According to the Vienna Convention on the Law of Treaties (VCLT), a treaty can be defined as:

> "*... an international agreement concluded between States in written form and governed by international law, whether embodied in a single instrument or in two or more related instruments and whatever its particular designation.*"[1]

7. The annex to the report on Action 15 draws on the work of the informal group of experts on the multilateral instrument[2] set up by the CFA to advise on the feasibility of a multilateral instrument to implement BEPS measures. The group was comprised of thirteen experts in public international law or international taxation from both civil and common law countries.

8. It is important to underline that the annex has been prepared in parallel to the discussions on the substance of the possible BEPS measures and that the experts have not participated in those intergovernmental discussions.

9. Accordingly, this annex offers a toolbox of theoretical options which could be used, as appropriate, in the development of a multilateral instrument. The options presented are based solely on an analysis of doctrine and precedents in public international law and should not be seen in any way as concrete proposals for the future multilateral instrument on BEPS.

10. The examples set out in the annex deliberately offer a vast array of options so that the drafters of a future multilateral instrument can pick and choose the solutions which are most appropriate for their purposes. As with any toolbox, it is not possible to use all of the tools at the same time. Moreover, the examples necessarily come from a wide range of subject areas and may have to be adapted to the specificities of the area of taxation.

11. The present annex is structured around three key issues that work on the multilateral instrument will need to address: (1) how to modify the network of bilateral tax treaties; (2) possibilities for providing the appropriate flexibility in States' level of commitment in order to enable effective coordination to tackle BEPS while preserving State sovereignty in tax matters; and (3) how to ensure transparency and clarity for all stakeholders. As set out below, there are various options for the multilateral instrument to fulfil each of these objectives, based on the law of treaties as well as existing precedents in various fields of international law.

A.1. A multilateral instrument can modify the network of bilateral tax treaties[3]

12. The primary objective of the multilateral instrument would be to implement the measures agreed in order to address BEPS, thereby modifying the existing network of bilateral tax treaties. At the outset, it is important to note that public international law allows various options for the modification of treaties as long as the principle of sovereignty and State consent is respected. Accordingly, if the parties agree, a treaty can be modified in a number of different ways, including through the adoption of a subsequent multilateral agreement, as envisaged here.

A.1.1. Terminology: "Modification" is more appropriate than "amendment"

13. The underlying goal of the BEPS Project is to develop and implement new common rules to tackle BEPS among all interested parties. The multilateral instrument need not and would not terminate the pre-existing network of bilateral treaties in order to achieve this goal. Instead it would aim to achieve a concurrent and integrated application of the provisions of the multilateral instrument and the bilateral treaties as they relate to BEPS. The bilateral treaties will not only remain in force but they will continue to play a major role in defining the specific relations of each pair of parties with regard to co-operation in tax matters.

14. Under international law, the basic principle is that a subsequent treaty prevails over a previously concluded treaty on the same subject matter. Accordingly, without formally amending each and every bilateral treaty, a new multilateral instrument would operate to modify the overlapping provisions in all bilateral treaties. Indeed, there have been a number of situations in which States have adopted multilateral conventions in order to introduce common international rules and standards and thereby harmonise a network of bilateral treaties, for example, in the area of extradition.

15. Accordingly, the term "modification" is better adapted to this project than the term "amendment". There is no need for a formal "amendment" of each one of the existing bilateral tax treaties. Rather, these treaties will be "modified" automatically by the multilateral instrument.

A.1.2 Relationship between the multilateral instrument and bilateral tax treaties

16. In the present case, it is foreseen that only certain provisions of the bilateral tax treaties will be modified and superseded by the multilateral instrument. Therefore the substantive rules contained in the bilateral tax treaties will remain in force in areas not covered by the multilateral instrument.

A.1.2.1 Bilateral tax treaties concluded prior to the entry into force of the multilateral instrument

17. There are two ways to address the question of the relationship between a multilateral instrument and the bilateral treaties modified by it: (1) to explicitly define this relationship in the multilateral instrument or (2) to let this relationship be defined by the general rules of international law.

18. In the silence of the multilateral treaty, the applicable customary rule, codified in Article 30(3) of the VCLT,[4] is that when two rules apply to the same matter, the later in time prevails (*lex posterior derogat legi priori*). Accordingly, earlier (i.e. previously concluded) bilateral treaties would continue to apply only to the extent that their provisions are compatible with those of the later multilateral treaty.

19. However, in order to preserve clarity and transparency, it would be important to explicitly define the relationship between the multilateral instrument and the existing network of bilateral treaties. This can be done through the inclusion of compatibility clauses in the multilateral instrument.

i. The rationale for compatibility clauses

20. When treaties are negotiated in areas where other treaties already exist, it is common practice to include a compatibility clause (or "conflict clause") to explicitly address the relationship between the treaties. This has been done in several other cases in which the provisions of a multilateral instrument have superseded the provisions of an existing network of bilateral treaties, particularly when the subject matter is complex (see below).

21. In the present case, given the number of bilateral treaties concerned and the technical nature of their content, it would be preferable to have an express provision in the multilateral instrument to define its relationship with existing bilateral treaties. If the parties agree, a mechanism could also be set up to resolve issues related to the implementation of the compatibility clause.

22. This would ensure clarity and transparency for all stakeholders (national administrations, tax services, domestic judges, taxpayers, civil society, etc.) on the fact that, in principle, the provisions of the multilateral instrument are to be applied in case of conflict with pre-existing rules of the bilateral treaties.

ii. Types of compatibility clause

23. The practice is diverse and there is no standard compatibility clause. In the precedents described below, multilateral instruments have "abrogated", "replaced", "superseded" and/ or "modified" the provisions of pre-existing bilateral treaties. In one example, the provisions of the multilateral instrument have been "included" in the bilateral treaties. The level of precision and the extent of changes made to the bilateral treaties vary.

24. In the following examples, it is important to note that the bilateral treaty survives, either in areas not addressed by the provisions of the multilateral instrument or as between a party to the multilateral instrument and a third party both of whom are parties to a previously concluded treaty (see section A.1.3 below).

- The multilateral instrument supersedes the provisions of bilateral treaties which cover the same specific subject matter as the multilateral instrument.

European **Convention on Extradition (1957)**

Article 28(1) – Relations between this Convention and bilateral Agreements: "*This Convention shall, in respect of those countries to which it applies, supersede the provisions of any bilateral treaties, conventions or agreements governing extradition between any two Contracting Parties.*"

European Convention on the Repatriation of Minors (1970)

Article 27(1): "*Subject to the provisions of paragraphs 3 and 4 of this article, this Convention shall, in respect of the territories to which it applies, supersede the provisions of any treaties, conventions or bilateral agreements between Contracting States governing the repatriation of minors for the reasons specified in Article 2, to the extent that the Contracting States may always avail themselves of the facilities for repatriation provided for in this Convention.*"

- The multilateral instrument modifies the provisions of pre-existing (bilateral or other) treaties only in so far as they differ from or are incompatible with the provisions of the multilateral instrument. There are various thresholds for the invocation of these compatibility clauses: in some cases, any difference will suffice ("at variance"), while others require inconsistency or incompatibility between the provisions.

European Convention on the Suppression of Terrorism (1977)

Article 8(3): "*The provisions of all treaties and arrangements concerning mutual assistance in criminal matters applicable between Contracting States, including the European Convention on Mutual Assistance in Criminal Matters, are modified as between Contracting States to the extent that they are incompatible with this Convention.*"

North American Free Trade Agreement (1994)

Article 103 – Relation to Other Agreements: "*1. The Parties affirm their existing rights and obligations with respect to each other under the General Agreement on Tariffs and Trade and other agreements to which such Parties are party. 2. In the event of any inconsistency between this Agreement and such other agreements, this Agreement shall prevail to the extent of the inconsistency, except as otherwise provided in this Agreement.*"

International Convention for the Suppression of the Financing of Terrorism (1999)

Article 11(5): "*The provisions of all extradition treaties and arrangements between States Parties with regard to offences set forth in article 2 shall be deemed to be modified as between States Parties to the extent that they are incompatible with this Convention.*"

- There are also cases in which the compatibility clause, while providing for the primacy of the multilateral instrument over pre-existing (bilateral or other) treaties, explains that the rights and obligations arising from these other treaties are not affected by the multilateral instrument to the extent that they are compatible with the multilateral instrument. The first example is noteworthy: the multilateral instrument stipulates that its provisions supersede those of pre-existing treaties but explicitly provides that obligations in pre-existing treaties on issues not addressed by the multilateral instrument continue to apply.

European Convention on Mutual Assistance in Criminal Matters (1959)

Article 26: "*1. Subject to the provisions of Article 15, paragraph 7, and Article 16, paragraph 3, this Convention shall, in respect of those countries to which it applies, supersede the provisions of any treaties, conventions or bilateral agreements governing mutual assistance in criminal matters between any two Contracting Parties. 2. This Convention shall not affect obligations incurred under the terms of any other bilateral or multilateral international convention which contains or may contain clauses governing specific aspects of mutual assistance in a given field.*"

United Nations Convention on the Law of the Sea (1982)

Article 311(2) – Relation to other conventions and international agreements: "*This Convention shall not alter the rights and obligations of States Parties which arise from other agreements compatible with this Convention and which do not affect the enjoyment by other States Parties of their rights or the performance of their obligations under this Convention* [...]"

- A variant is the case when the multilateral instrument creates an exception to a general principle that the provisions of the multilateral instrument supersede those of prior agreements, by providing that "more favourable" provisions of a bilateral or multilateral treaty existing at the time of the conclusion of the multilateral instrument shall not be affected.

Convention for the Elimination of All Forms of Discrimination Against Women (1979)

Article 23: "*Nothing in the present Convention shall affect any provisions that are more conducive to the achievement of equality between men and women which may be contained:* [...] *(b) In any other international convention, treaty or agreement in force for that State.*"

International Convention on the Protection of the Rights of All Migrant Workers and Members of their Families (1990)

Article 81(1): "*Nothing in the present Convention shall affect more favourable rights or freedoms granted to migrant workers and members of their families by virtue of:* [...] *(b) Any bilateral or multilateral treaty in force for the State Party concerned.*"

- Finally, in some cases, the multilateral treaty goes further and clearly indicates which of its provisions are added to the bilateral instruments or which provisions of the bilateral treaties are modified and how. The following example concerns the addition by a multilateral treaty to a list of offences defined as extraditable in bilateral treaties.

Convention for the Suppression of Unlawful Acts against the Safety of Maritime Navigation (1988)

Article 11(1): "[*t*]*he offences set forth in article 3 shall be deemed to be included as extraditable offences in any extradition treaty existing between any of the States Parties.*"

iii. Compatibility clauses can address complex situations

25. A compatibility clause can take into account variations of scope, wording and paragraph numbering between bilateral treaties modified by the multilateral instrument. Careful drafting of the clause can circumvent the potential issues that could arise from those variations.

26. There are useful precedents in which the compatibility clause in the multilateral instrument describes:

- The provisions to be modified by using a precise description which removes the necessity to refer to a specific provision or paragraph number in the bilateral treaties.
- The exact effect of its provisions on those of bilateral treaties, through the inclusion of connecting terms such as "in place of", "in addition to", "in the absence of".

Agreement on extradition between the European Union and the United States of America (2003)[5]

Article 3(1) – Scope of application of this Agreement in relation to bilateral extradition treaties with Member States: "*The European Union, pursuant to the Treaty on European Union, and the United States of America shall ensure that the provisions of this Agreement are applied in relation to bilateral extradition treaties between the Member States and the United States of America, in force at the time of the entry into force of this Agreement, under the following terms:*

(a) Article 4 shall be applied in place of bilateral treaty provisions that authorise extradition exclusively with respect to a list of specified criminal offences;

(b) Article 5 shall be applied in place of bilateral treaty provisions governing transmission, certification, authentication or legalisation of an extradition request and supporting documents transmitted by the requesting State;

(c) Article 6 shall be applied in the absence of bilateral treaty provisions authorising direct transmission of provisional arrest requests between the United States Department of Justice and the Ministry of Justice of the Member State concerned;

(d) Article 7 shall be applied in addition to bilateral treaty provisions governing transmission of extradition requests;

(e) Article 8 shall be applied in the absence of bilateral treaty provisions governing the submission of supplementary information; where bilateral treaty provisions do not specify the channel to be used, paragraph 2 of that Article shall also be applied;

(f) Article 9 shall be applied in the absence of bilateral treaty provisions authorising temporary surrender of persons being proceeded against or serving a sentence in the requested State;

(g) Article 10 shall be applied, except as otherwise specified therein, in place of, or in the absence of, bilateral treaty provisions pertaining to decision on several requests for extradition of the same person;

(h) Article 11 shall be applied in the absence of bilateral treaty provisions authorising waiver of extradition or simplified extradition procedures;

(i) Article 12 shall be applied in the absence of bilateral treaty provisions governing transit; where bilateral treaty provisions do not specify the procedure governing unscheduled landing of aircraft, paragraph 3 of that Article shall also be applied;

(j) Article 13 may be applied by the requested State in place of, or in the absence of, bilateral treaty provisions governing capital punishment;

(k) Article 14 shall be applied in the absence of bilateral treaty provisions governing treatment of sensitive information in a request."

A.1.2.2. Bilateral tax treaties concluded after the entry into force of the multilateral instrument

27. In order to ensure consistency with the legal regime established by the multilateral instrument, the parties might deem it necessary to define certain parameters for their future treaty-making activities through a forward looking compatibility or "obedience" clause.

28. Compatibility or obedience clauses, which are included in a number of existing multilateral treaties, stipulate that parties shall not conclude subsequent agreements which are in contradiction with the treaty.

29. In some cases, the objective of subsequent agreements by two or more parties to a multilateral instrument may be to go further than the content of the main agreement by establishing a "special regime" between themselves. This is the scenario addressed and codified by article 41 of the VCLT.[6] According to this article, subsequent agreements must not be prohibited by the main agreement and must not affect the rights and obligations of other parties to the treaty.

- Multilateral instruments may include clauses which allow parties to take on more far reaching commitments with other parties on the condition that the subsequent agreements can only confirm, supplement, extend or amplify the provisions of the main multilateral treaty.

European Convention on Extradition (1957)

Article 28(2) – Relations between this Convention and bilateral Agreements: "*The Contracting Parties may conclude between themselves bilateral or multilateral agreements only in order to supplement the provisions of this Convention or to facilitate the application of the principles contained therein.*"

Vienna Convention on Consular Relations (1963)

Article 73(2) – Relationship between the present Convention and other international agreements: "*Nothing in the present Convention shall preclude States from concluding international agreements confirming or supplementing or extending or amplifying the provisions thereof*".

- Multilateral instruments can also take the opposite approach providing that any subsequent agreements must not run contrary to the object and purpose of the main treaty or be inconsistent with its provisions.

Chicago Convention on International Civil Aviation (1944)

Article 83 – Registration of new arrangements: "*Subject to the provisions of the preceding Article, any contracting State may make arrangements not inconsistent with the provisions of this Convention. Any such arrangement shall be forthwith registered with the Council, which shall make it public as soon as possible*".

United Nations Convention on the Law of the Sea (1982)

Article 311(3) – Relation to other conventions and international agreements: "*Two or more States Parties may conclude agreements modifying or suspending the operation of provisions of this Convention, applicable solely to the relations between them, provided that such agreements do not relate to a provision derogation from which is incompatible with the effective execution of the object and purpose of this Convention, and provided further that such agreements shall not affect the application of the basic principles embodied herein, and that the provisions of such agreements do not affect the enjoyment by other States Parties of their rights or the performance of their obligations under this Convention.*"

Council of Europe Convention on the Prevention of Terrorism (2005)

Article 26(2) – Effects of the Convention: "[...] *However, where Parties establish their relations in respect of the matters dealt with in the present Convention other than as regulated therein, they shall do so in a manner that is not inconsistent with the Convention's objectives and principles.*"

- Finally, in some cases the multilateral treaty may even invite parties to adopt subsequent agreements in order to go further than the main treaty or facilitate its effective application.

United Nations Convention Against Transnational Organized Crime and the Protocols Thereto (2000)

Article 19 – Joint investigations: "*State Parties shall consider concluding bilateral or multilateral agreements or arrangements whereby, in relation to matters that are the subject of investigations, prosecutions or judicial proceedings in one or more States, the competent authorities concerned may establish joint investigative bodies.* [...]"

A.1.3 Relationship between parties to the multilateral instrument and third parties

30. A corollary of the principle of State sovereignty is that treaties are only binding on the parties.[7]

> "*A treaty does not create either obligations or rights for a third State without its consent*"[8] and "[*a*]*n obligation arises for a third State from a provision of a treaty if the parties to the treaty intend the provision to be the means of establishing the obligation and the third State expressly accepts that obligation in writing.*"[9] (emphasis added)

31. Accordingly, in the present case, the content of the multilateral instrument would not be binding on third parties (i.e. States which are not parties to the instrument). A party to the multilateral instrument and a third party would continue to be bound by the provisions of any bilateral tax treaty concluded between themselves without the modifications set out in the multilateral instrument. It would however be possible to include a variant of the compatibility clause which would request the parties to take into account as far as possible the provisions of the multilateral instrument when negotiating bilateral tax treaties with third parties. The multilateral instrument could also create the possibility for the parties to confer regarding any issues that may be raised by third parties over time.

A.1.4 Timeline for entry into force of the multilateral instrument

A.1.4.1 Entry into force of the instrument and its provisions

i. The date of the "entry into force" of the instrument

32. The negotiating States can decide at what date and under which conditions the instrument would enter into force, for example, after a certain number of ratifications. The instrument would then be in effect but would only bind those States which have already ratified by that date. Naturally the modalities for the implementation of the multilateral instrument in each State would depend on its constitutional system.

Convention on Mutual Administrative Assistance in Tax Matters (1988)

Article 28(2) – Signature and entry into force of the Convention: "*This Convention shall enter into force on the first day of the month following the expiration of a period of three months after the date on which five States have expressed their consent to be bound by the Convention in accordance with the provisions of paragraph 1.*"

ii. The "start date" of the different measures provided for in the instrument

33. Clauses in the multilateral instrument can specify a start date for the various measures foreseen. It is possible to specify different dates for different provisions of the treaty to take effect (e.g. a fixed period after the entry into force of the treaty for withholding taxes and the start of the tax year in each country for other taxes).

34. The fact that the start of a tax year may be different in each State is not an obstacle. For example, certain measures could take effect at the start of the next tax year in each country following the entry into force of the treaty for that country (or provide for other practical and flexible solutions).

Convention on Mutual Administrative Assistance in Tax Matters (1988)

Article 28(6) – Signature and entry into force of the Convention: "*The provisions of this Convention, as amended by the 2010 Protocol, shall have effect for administrative assistance related to taxable periods beginning on or after 1 January of the year following the one in which the Convention, as amended by the 2010 Protocol, entered into force in respect of a Party, or where there is no taxable period, for administrative assistance related to charges to tax arising on or after 1 January of the year following the one in which the Convention, as amended by the 2010 Protocol, entered into force in respect of a Party. Any two or more Parties may mutually agree that the Convention, as amended by the 2010 Protocol, shall have effect for administrative assistance related to earlier taxable periods or charges to tax.*"

Agreement among the Governments of the Member States of the Caribbean Community for the Avoidance of Double Taxation and the Prevention of Fiscal Evasion with Respect to Taxes on Income, Profits, or Gains and Capital Gains and for the Encouragement of Regional Trade and Investment (1994)

Article 28 – Entry Into Force: "*1. This Agreement shall enter into force on the deposit of the second instrument of ratification in accordance with Article 27 and shall there upon take effect*

(a) in respect of taxes withheld at the source, on amounts paid or credited to a person, on the first day of the calendar month next following the month of deposit of the second instrument of ratification;

(b) in respect of other taxes, for taxable years beginning on or after the first day of January next following the deposit of the second instrument of ratification.

Convention on Mutual Administrative Assistance in Tax Matters (1988) *(continued)*

2. Where a State ratifies this Agreement after it was entered into force, the Agreement shall take effect in relation to that State

(a) in respect of the taxes mentioned in paragraph 1(a), on the first day of the calendar month next following the deposit of its instrument of ratification;

(b) in respect of other taxes, for the taxable years beginning on or after the first day of January next following the deposit of its instrument of ratification."

A.1.4.2 Entry into force for a party joining subsequently

35. The instrument can specify modalities for its entry into force for jurisdictions that become parties after the entry into force of the instrument itself. The default position would be entry into force upon deposit of instrument of ratification/accession but there can be a time lapse, if necessary, in order to deal with potential technical difficulties.

Convention on Mutual Administrative Assistance in Tax Matters (1988)

Article 28(5) – Signature and entry into force of the Convention: "[...] *In respect of any State ratifying the Convention as amended by the 2010 Protocol in accordance with this paragraph, this Convention shall enter into force on the first day of the month following the expiration of a period of three months after the date of deposit of the instrument of ratification with one of the Depositaries.*"

36. The provisions on the start date for certain provisions, for example those which would take effect at the start of the next tax year, could also apply to jurisdictions which become parties to the multilateral instrument after its entry into force.

A.1.5 Ensuring consistency in the interpretation and implementation of the multilateral instrument

A.1.5.1. The instrument could be accompanied by interpretative guidance

37. Many treaties are accompanied by commentaries, agreed by all parties, providing background information and guidance as to the meaning of provisions and modalities of implementation (e.g. the *Explanatory Report to the Convention on Mutual Administrative Assistance in Tax Matters,*[10] hereafter "MAC"). The relationship between the treaty and its commentaries could be defined in the provisions of the treaty itself.

A.1.5.2 Discussions between the parties on implementation

38. If agreed by the parties, a Conference of Parties or a Co-ordinating Body could be given responsibility for discussing questions related to the instrument, or for monitoring its implementation.

Convention on International Trade in Endangered Species of Wild Fauna and Flora (1973)

Article 11 – Conference of the Parties: "*1. The Secretariat shall call a meeting of the Conference of the Parties not later than two years after the entry into force of the present Convention. 2. Thereafter the Secretariat shall convene regular meetings at least once every two years, unless the Conference decides otherwise, and extraordinary meetings at any time on the written request of at least one-third of the Parties. 3. At meetings, whether regular or extraordinary, the Parties shall review the implementation of the present Convention and may:(a) make such provision as may be necessary to enable the Secretariat to carry out its duties, and adopt financial provisions;(b) consider and adopt amendments to Appendices I and II in accordance with Article XV;(c) review the progress made towards the restoration and conservation of the species included in Appendices I, II and III;(d) receive and consider any reports presented by the Secretariat or by any Party; and (e) where appropriate, make recommendations for improving the effectiveness of the present Convention.*"

Convention on Mutual Administrative Assistance in Tax Matters (1988)

Article 24(3) – Implementation of the Convention: "*A co-ordinating body composed of representatives of the competent authorities of the Parties shall monitor the implementation and development of this Convention, under the aegis of the OECD. To that end, the co-ordinating body shall recommend any action likely to further the general aims of the Convention. In particular it shall act as a forum for the study of new methods and procedures to increase international co-operation in tax matters and, where appropriate, it may recommend revisions or amendments to the Convention. States which have signed but not yet ratified, accepted or approved the Convention are entitled to be represented at the meetings of the co-ordinating body as observers.*"

39. If the parties so wish, more specific questions, such as the implementation of compatibility clauses with respect to pre-existing bilateral treaties, could be addressed by providing in the multilateral instrument for mechanisms such as consultation procedures, which exist in most bilateral tax treaties, to resolve any difficulty:

Nordic Mutual Assistance Convention on Mutual Administrative Assistance in Tax Matters (1989)

Article 20 – Special provisions: "*2. If difficulties or doubts arise between two or more of the Contracting States regarding the interpretation or application of this Convention, the competent authorities of these States consult together to resolve the issue by special agreement. The outcome of such consultations shall be communicated to the competent authorities of the other Contracting States without delay. 3. If the competent authority of one of the Contracting States is of the opinion that consultations regarding a question referred to in paragraph 2 should take place between the competent authorities of all Contracting States, such consultations shall take place at the request of that State.*"

United Nations Framework Convention on Climate Change (1992)

Article 13 – Resolution of questions regarding implementation: "*The Conference of the Parties shall, at its first session, consider the establishment of a multilateral consultative process, available to Parties on their request, for the resolution of questions regarding the implementation of the Convention.*"

South Asian Association for Regional Cooperation (SAARC) Limited Multilateral Agreement on Avoidance of Double Taxation and Mutual Administrative Assistance in Tax Matters (2005)

Article 12 – Implementation: "*The Member States shall hold periodic consultations, as appropriate, of Competent Authorities, with a view to facilitating the effective implementation of this Agreement.*"

A.1.6 Possibility for expeditious and consensual amendment of the multilateral instrument

40. The general rule, codified in Article 39 of the VCLT is that treaties can be amended "by agreement between the parties". It is important to note that "the amending agreement does not bind any State already a Party to the treaty which does not become a Party to the amending agreement".[11]

41. Given the nature of this multilateral instrument, it will be particularly important that the mechanism of amendment is efficient but, at the same time, respects sovereign prerogatives and ensures that parties will only be bound by amendments to which they have consented.

Convention on the Prohibition of the Use, Stockpiling, Production and Transfer of Anti-Personnel Mines and on their Destruction (1997)

Article 13(5) – Amendments: "*An amendment to this Convention shall enter into force for all States Parties to this Convention, which have accepted it, upon the deposit with the Depositary of instruments of acceptance by a majority of States Parties. Thereafter it shall enter into force for any remaining State Party on the date of deposit of its instrument of acceptance.*"

United Nations Convention against Transnational Organized Crime (2000)

Article 39(5) – Amendment: "*When an amendment enters into force, it shall be binding on those States Parties which have expressed their consent to be bound by it. Other States Parties shall still be bound by the provisions of this Convention and any earlier amendments that they have ratified, accepted or approved.*"

A.2. A multilateral instrument can provide flexibility in the level of commitment

42. Given that the objective of the multilateral instrument is to harmonise the approaches to BEPS and create a level playing field, it will be important to ensure that the commitments of the parties are as aligned as possible. However, it is possible for the multilateral instrument to provide flexibility if there are specific cases where certain tax policies that cannot be harmonised amongst all parties to the multilateral instrument and the level of commitment the parties are prepared to undertake depends on the partner jurisdiction.

A.2.1 Two types of flexibility in the level of commitment

A.2.1.1 Level of commitment vis-à-vis all other parties (i.e. on the substance of specific provisions)

43. There are various ways to ensure flexibility in the substantive commitments made vis-à-vis all parties.

- First, it would be possible for parties to exclude the application, in full or in part, of certain provisions.
- Second, parties could be given a choice between alternative measures set out in the instrument.
- Third, the multilateral instrument could foresee the possibility for parties to take on additional commitments including through an optional protocol to the main treaty, in areas where this would not interfere with the overarching objective of addressing BEPS in a co-ordinated way.

44. These possibilities are described in more detail in section A.2.2 below.

A.2.1.2 Level of commitment vis-à-vis certain parties (i.e. depending on the partner jurisdiction)

45. As shown by the variations present in the existing network of bilateral tax treaties, parties may not be ready to accept the same level of commitment vis-à-vis all other parties. It is possible for the instrument to allow parties to modulate their level of commitment depending on the partner jurisdiction in question.

46. One option would be for certain provisions of the multilateral instrument to explicitly foresee different levels of commitment (alternative provisions – see below section A.2.2.2.) and a system of notifications as to the level of commitment accepted vis-à-vis different parties. A new notification would be necessary each time that another jurisdiction becomes party to the treaty.

General Agreement on Tariffs and Trade (1947)

Article XXXV – Non-application of the Agreement between Particular Contracting Parties: "*1. This Agreement, or alternatively Article II of this Agreement, shall not apply as between any contracting party and any other contracting party if: (a) the two contracting parties have not entered into tariff negotiations with each other, and (b) either of the contracting parties, at the time either becomes a contracting party, does not consent to such application. 2. The Contracting Parties may review the operation of this Article in particular cases at the request of any contracting party and make appropriate recommendations.*"

47. A related issue is the situation of parties bound by a regional regime. If appropriate, the multilateral instrument could allow for such parties to apply a specific regime between themselves if certain conditions are met. This can be through the use of a so-called "disconnection clause", which has been used with regard to the European Union (EU).

A.2.2 Modalities for introducing flexibility in the multilateral instrument

48. This section develops the modalities for introducing flexibility in the level of substantive commitments, as set out in section A.2.1 above.

49. Parties could commit to a core set of provisions in the multilateral instrument but could have the possibility to opt-out of certain measures, choose between alternative – clearly delineated – measures and/or opt-in to additional measures. All of these mechanisms could be used as appropriate for different provisions of the multilateral instrument. Finally, flexibility could be introduced through the wording used and the type of obligations contained in the provisions of the multilateral instrument.

50. Opt-in and opt-out mechanisms are well-known devices to ensure flexibility and are a standard technique used in treaties developed within several international organisations, including the International Labour Organisation (ILO) and International Civil Aviation Organisation (ICAO).[12]

A.2.2.1 Opt-out mechanisms

51. Parties are permitted to exclude or modify the legal effect of certain provisions, in whole or in part, through the use of explicit opt-out mechanisms foreseen by the treaty, the formulation of reservations, or the use of other mechanisms such as derogations, waivers and restrictions.

> *"According to a widely accepted definition, an exclusionary or opting-out (or contracting-out) clause is a treaty provision by which a State will be bound by rules contained in the treaty unless it expresses its intent not to be bound, within a certain period of time, by some of those provisions."*[13]

- There are many precedents of explicit opt-out mechanisms, in particular in the treaties adopted under the auspices of the ILO and the Council of Europe. Opt-out mechanisms can be limited to a defined period of time.

International Labour Convention No. 63 concerning statistics of wages and hours of work (1938)

Article 2(1): *"Any Member which ratifies this Convention may, by a declaration appended to its ratification, exclude from its acceptance of the Convention: (a) any one of Parts II, III or IV; or (b) Parts II and IV; or (c) Parts III and IV."*

Convention for the Prevention of Pollution from Ships (1973)

Article 14(1): *"A State may, at the time of signing, ratifying, accepting, approving or acceding to the present Convention, declare that it does not accept any one or all of Annexes III, IV and V (hereinafter referred to as 'Optional Annexes') of the present Convention. Subject to the above, Parties to the Convention shall be bound by any Annex in its entirety."*

Statute of the International Criminal Court (1998)

Article 124 – Transitional Provision: *"Notwithstanding article 12, paragraphs 1 and 2, a State, on becoming a party to this Statute, may declare that, for a period of seven years after the entry into force of this Statute for the State concerned, it does not accept the jurisdiction of the Court with respect to the category of crimes referred to in article 8 when a crime is alleged to have been committed by its nationals or on its territory. A declaration under this article may be withdrawn at any time. The provisions of this article shall be reviewed at the Review Conference convened in accordance with article 123, paragraph 1."*

- Even in cases where this type of explicit opt-out mechanism is not present, the formulation of reservations allows the possibility to opt-out from some provisions of a treaty.

A reservation is defined as a unilateral statement made by a State, when signing, ratifying, accepting, approving or acceding to a multilateral instrument, whereby it purports to exclude or to modify the legal effect of certain provisions of the Convention (cf. Articles 19 to 23 of the VCLT). To be permissible, a reservation should not be prohibited by the treaty and should not be incompatible with its object and purpose.

If the multilateral instrument is silent, it would in principle be possible for parties to formulate reservations to any of its substantive provisions. However, in the interests of preventing opting-out from core provisions, the multilateral instrument could allow the formulation of reservations only for certain provisions by setting out an exhaustive list of permitted reservations.

Convention on Mutual Administrative Assistance in Tax Matters (1988)

Article 30 – Reservations: "*1. Any State may, at the time of signature or when depositing its instrument of ratification, acceptance or approval or at any later date, declare that it reserves the right:*

a. not to provide any form of assistance in relation to the taxes of other Parties in any of the categories listed in sub-paragraph b. of paragraph 1 of Article 2, provided that it has not included any domestic tax in that category under Annex A of the Convention;

b. not to provide assistance in the recovery of any tax claim, or in the recovery of an administrative fine, for all taxes or only for taxes in one or more of the categories listed in paragraph 1 of Article 2;

c. not to provide assistance in respect of any tax claim, which is in existence at the date of entry into force of the Convention in respect of that State or, where a reservation has previously been made under sub-paragraph a. or b. above, at the date of withdrawal of such a reservation in relation to taxes in the category in question;

d. not to provide assistance in the service of documents for all taxes or only for taxes in one or more of the categories listed in paragraph 1 of Article 2;

e. not to permit the service of documents through the post as provided for in paragraph 3 of Article 17;

f. to apply paragraph 7 of Article 28 exclusively for administrative assistance related to taxable periods beginning on or after 1 January of the third year preceding the one in which the Convention, as amended by the 2010 Protocol, entered into force in respect of a Party, or where there is no taxable period, for administrative assistance related to charges to tax arising on or after 1 January of the third year preceding the one in which the Convention, as amended by the 2010 Protocol, entered into force in respect of a Party.

2. No other reservation may be made."

Convention on Cybercrime (2001)

Article 9 (4) – Offences related to child pornography: "*Each Party may reserve the right not to apply, in whole or in part, paragraphs 1, sub-paragraphs d and e, and 2, subparagraphs b and c*" to be read in connection with Article 42 – Reservations: "*By a written notification addressed to the Secretary General of the Council of Europe, any State may, at the time of signature or when depositing its instrument of ratification, acceptance, approval or accession, declare that it avails itself of the reservation(s) provided for in Article 4, paragraph 2, Article 6, paragraph 3, Article 9, paragraph 4, Article 10, paragraph 3, Article 11, paragraph 3, Article 14, paragraph 3, Article 22, paragraph 2, Article 29, paragraph 4, and Article 41, paragraph 1. No other reservation may be made.*"

A.2.2.2 Choice between alternative provisions

52. Parties could be given the choice:

i. Between specific alternative provisions (either/or)

General Act for Conciliation, Judicial Settlement and Arbitration (1928)

Article 38(1): "*Accessions to the present General Act may extend: A. Either to all the provisions of the Act (chapters I, II, III and IV); B. Or to those provisions only which relate to conciliation and judicial settlement (chapters I and II), together with the general provisions dealing with these procedures (Chapter IV).*"

ILO Convention No. 96 (revised) concerning Fee-Charging Employment Agencies (1949)

Article 2(1): "*Each Member ratifying this Convention shall indicate in its instrument of ratification whether it accepts the provisions of part II of the Convention, providing for the progressive abolition of fee-charging employment agencies conducted with a view to profit and the regulation of other agencies, or the provisions of part III, providing for the regulation of fee-charging employment agencies including agencies conducted with a view to profit.*"

ii. Among a list of provisions with a defined minimum

Convention No. 102 concerning Minimum Standards of Social Security (1952)

Article 2: "*Each Member for which this Convention is in force: (a) shall comply with: (i) Part I; (ii) at least three of Parts II, III, IV, V, VI, VII, VIII, IX and X, including at least one of Parts IV, V, VI, IX and X; (iii) the relevant provisions of Parts XI, XII and XIII; and (iv) Part XIV.*"

European Social Charter (1961)

Article 20(1) – Undertakings: "*Each of the Contracting Parties undertakes: (a) To consider part I of this Charter as a declaration of the aims which it will pursue by all appropriate means, as stated in the introductory paragraph of that part; (b) To consider itself bound by at least five of the following articles of part II of this Charter: Articles 1, 5, 6, 12, 13, 16 and 19; (c)* [...] *to consider itself bound by such a number of articles or numbered paragraphs of part II of the Charter as it may select, provided that the total number of articles or numbered paragraphs by which it is bound is not less than 10 articles or 45 numbered paragraphs.*"

European Charter for Regional or Minority Languages (1992)

Article 2 – Undertakings: "*1. Each Party undertakes to apply the provisions of Part II to all the regional or minority languages spoken within its territory and which comply with the definition in Article 1. 2. In respect of each language specified at the time of ratification, acceptance or approval, in accordance with Article 3, each Party undertakes to apply a minimum of thirty-five paragraphs or sub-paragraphs chosen from among the provisions of Part III of the Charter, including at least three chosen from each of the Articles 8 and 12 and one from each of the Articles 9, 10, 11 and 13.*"

Bali Agreement on Trade Facilitation (2013)

Article 7.3. – Trade Facilitation Measures for Authorized Operators: "*The trade facilitation measures provided pursuant to paragraph 7.1 shall include at least 3 of the following measures: a. low documentary and data requirements as appropriate; b. low rate of physical inspections and examinations as appropriate; c. rapid release time as appropriate; d. deferred payment of duties, taxes, fees and charges; e. use of comprehensive guarantees or reduced guarantees; f. a single customs declaration for all imports or exports in a given period; and g. clearance of goods at the premises of the authorized operator or another place authorized by customs.*"

A.2.2.3 Opt-in mechanisms

53. Opt-in (or contracting-in) mechanisms are defined "as provisions stipulating that the parties to a treaty may accept obligations which, in the absence of explicit acceptance, would not be automatically applicable to them".[14] The goal of such mechanisms is to allow parties which are ready to do so to commit to further action in pursuit of the objectives of the treaty.

- When parties are given the choice between alternative provisions (see section A.2.2.2 above), they will opt-in to additional commitments if they go beyond the defined minimum number of commitments and choose to be bound by a larger set of provisions.
- Parties can also be offered the possibility to accept being bound by specific and clearly identified provisions through a unilateral declaration.

Hague Convention on the recognition and enforcement of decisions relating to maintenance obligations (1973)

Article 25: "*Any Contracting State may, at any time, declare that the provisions of this Convention will be extended, in relation to other States making a declaration under this Article, to an official deed ('acte authentique') drawn up by or before an authority or public official and directly enforceable in the State of origin insofar as these provisions can be applied to such deeds.*"

Energy Charter Treaty (1994)

Article 10(6) – Promotion, protection and treatment of investments: "*(a) A Contracting Party may, as regards the Making of Investments in its Area, at any time declare voluntarily to the Charter Conference, through the Secretariat, its intention not to introduce new exceptions to the Treatment described in paragraph (3). (b) A Contracting Party may, furthermore, at any time make a voluntary commitment to accord to Investors of other Contracting Parties, as regards the Making of Investments in some or all Economic Activities in the Energy Sector in its Area, the Treatment described in paragraph (3). Such commitments shall be notified to the Secretariat and listed in Annex VC and shall be binding under this Treaty.*"

International Covenant on Civil and Political Rights (1966)

Article 41(1): "*A State Party to the present Covenant may at any time declare under this article that it recognizes the competence of the Committee to receive and consider communications to the effect that a State Party claims that another State Party is not fulfilling its obligations under the present Covenant. Communications under this article may be received and considered only if submitted by a State Party which has made a declaration recognizing in regard to itself the competence of the Committee. No communication shall be received by the Committee if it concerns a State Party which has not made such a declaration.* [...]"

- Another way for parties to opt-in to additional commitments is through the conclusion of optional protocols to the multilateral instrument, which can be opened for signature at the same time or after the entry into force of the main treaty.

European Convention for the Protection of Human Rights and Fundamental Freedoms (1950)

Almost all Parties to the 1950 Convention have signed and ratified Protocol No. 6 to the Convention for the Protection of Human Rights and Fundamental Freedoms concerning the abolition of the death penalty (1983) which goes beyond the main instrument by stating that "death penalty shall be abolished" by the Parties.

Second Optional Protocol to the International Covenant on Civil and Political Rights, aiming at the abolition of the death penalty (1989)

Article 6: "*1. The provisions of the present Protocol shall apply as additional provisions to the Covenant. 2. Without prejudice to the possibility of a reservation under article 2 of the present Protocol, the right guaranteed in article 1, paragraph 1, of the present Protocol shall not be subject to any derogation under article 4 of the Covenant.*"

Article 7(1): "*The present Protocol is open for signature by any State that has signed the Covenant. 2. The present Protocol is subject to ratification by any State that has ratified the Covenant or acceded to it.* [...]"

Optional Protocol to the Convention on the Rights of the Child on the involvement of children in armed conflict (2000)

Article 9(1): "*The present Protocol is open for signature by any State that is a party to the Convention or has signed it.* [...]"

A.2.2.4 In-built flexibility in the formulation of provisions

54. Finally, the level of commitment of the parties with regard to specific provisions can depend on the wording used and on the type of obligations.

i. Wording

55. Within the same treaty, the level of commitment can be adjusted between different provisions and depending on the objective of a treaty:

- strong wording: "will", "shall", "must", "undertakes to"
- more flexible wording: "may", "as necessary/appropriate", "should consider", "take steps to", "with a view to", "including by".

Convention on Mutual Administrative Assistance in Tax Matters (1988)

Article 13 – Documents accompanying the request: "*1. The request for administrative assistance under this section shall be accompanied by:* [...]. *2. The instrument permitting enforcement of the applicant State* *shall, where appropriate and in accordance with the provisions in force in the requested State,* *be accepted, recognised, supplemented or replaced as soon as possible after the date of the receipt of the request for assistance, by an instrument permiting enforcement in the latter State.*"

United Nations Convention on the Law of the Sea (1982)

Article 123 – Cooperation of States bordering enclosed or semi-enclosed seas: "*States bordering an enclosed or semi-enclosed sea should cooperate with each other in the exercise of their rights and in the performance of their duties under this Convention. To this end they shall endeavour, directly or through an appropriate regional organization: (a) to coordinate the management, conservation, exploration and exploitation of the living resources of the sea; (b) to coordinate the implementation of their rights and duties with respect to the protection and preservation of the marine environment; (c) to coordinate their scientific research policies and undertake where appropriate joint programmes of scientific research in the area; (d) to invite, as appropriate, other interested States or international organizations to cooperate with them in furtherance of the provisions of this article.*"

ii. Type of obligations

56. It is also possible for different provisions to provide for different types of obligations:

- Obligations of result: parties are bound to achieve a particular outcome.

Convention on Access to Information, Public Participation in Decision-Making and Access to Justice in Environmental Matters (1998)

Article 1 – Objective: "*In order to contribute to the protection of the right of every person of present and future generations to live in an environment adequate to his or her health and well-being, each Party shall guarantee the rights of access to information, public participation in decision-making, and access to justice in environmental matters in accordance with the provisions of this Convention.*"

- Obligations of means/conduct: parties are bound to strive or endeavour to achieve an outcome.

> **United Nations Convention on the Law of the Sea (1982)**
>
> Article 194 – Measures to prevent, reduce and control pollution of the marine environment: "*1. States shall take, individually or jointly as appropriate, all measures consistent with this Convention that are necessary to prevent, reduce and control pollution of the marine environment from any source, using for this purpose the best practicable means at their disposal and in accordance with their capabilities, and they shall endeavour to harmonize their policies in this connection. 2. States shall take all measures necessary to ensure that activities under their jurisdiction or control are so conducted as not to cause damage by pollution to other States and their environment, and that pollution arising from incidents or activities under their jurisdiction or control does not spread beyond the areas where they exercise sovereign rights in accordance with this Convention.*"

- Or both: parties are bound to achieve a particular outcome in a particular way.

A.3. A multilateral instrument can ensure transparency and clarity of commitments

57. Given the practical consequences of changes to the rules in the field of international taxation, it is vital to ensure that the rights and obligations of parties to the multilateral instrument are clearly understood by all stakeholders, i.e. national tax administrations, taxpayers and third parties.

58. Beyond the publicity surrounding the work on BEPS and any resulting multilateral instrument, further steps will be needed to ensure that the modifications to existing bilateral tax treaties and the level of commitment undertaken by the parties are clear and transparent. A related question is differences in official languages between the bilateral tax treaties and the multilateral instrument. As set out below, there are various tools which could be used to address these issues.

59. The mechanisms described in section A.1.5 above to ensure consistency in interpretation and implementation (interpretative guidance, discussions between parties on implementation) will also be important in order to ensure transparency and clarity vis-à-vis all stakeholders.

A.3.1 Tools to ensure transparency and clarity

60. Different tools exist in order to ensure transparency and clarity of the commitments undertaken by parties to the multilateral instrument in two respects:

- First, on how the multilateral instrument has modified in concrete terms the provisions of existing bilateral tax treaties.
- Second, on the level of commitment undertaken by parties in cases where the multilateral instrument offers flexibility as described in section A.2 above.

A.3.1.1. Publication of consolidated versions

61. Consolidated versions of bilateral treaties could be prepared and published by parties in conjunction with the depositary of the multilateral instrument.

62. The consolidated version would reflect the concrete changes made to the existing bilateral tax treaty and, where appropriate, the level of commitment undertaken by parties in cases where the multilateral instrument allows defined flexibility. The formatting of the text could draw attention to the changes.

63. The preparation of the consolidated versions would be for transparency purposes and would not affect the date of legal effect of the modifications to the bilateral treaties which would be the date of the entry into force of the multilateral instrument.

64. In order to provide the necessary information to all relevant stakeholders, the consolidated versions of the bilateral tax treaties could be included in publicly accessible databases.

A.3.1.2 Notifications and communications

65. The depositary of the multilateral instrument can play a key role since it is in charge of "*receiving and keeping custody of any instruments, notifications and communications*"[15] relating to the treaty as well as of "*informing the parties and the States entitled to become parties to the treaty of acts, notifications and communications relating to the treaty*".[16]

i. Notifications by the parties to the depositary of the multilateral instrument

66. Notifications could contain information related to:

- modifications of the provisions of the bilateral tax treaties

  As an alternative to consolidated versions of bilateral tax treaties, it would be possible to require written notifications to the depositary of the multilateral instrument by the parties to bilateral treaties setting out the effect of the entry into force of the multilateral instrument on the application of the provisions of the bilateral treaty.

Agreement on extradition between the European Union and the United States of America (2003)

Article 3(2): "*(a) The European Union, pursuant to the Treaty on European Union, shall ensure that each Member State acknowledges, in a written instrument between such Member State and the United States of America, the application, in the manner set forth in this Article, of its bilateral extradition treaty in force with the United States of America.*"

- level of commitment undertaken by the parties.

  In certain cases, for example for reservations, it is well-established that these opt-out measures are communicated to the depositary which then notifies all parties to the treaty. The depositaries can also be asked to notify all or certain communications to a larger group than the parties to the treaty.

The same method could be adopted for other opt-out, choice of alternative provisions and opt-in measures. Accordingly, the multilateral instrument could specify that, upon ratification, each party must communicate the necessary information on all such measures to the depositary which will duly notify all parties.

United Nations Convention on the Law of the Sea (1982)

Article 311(4) – Relation to other conventions and international agreements: "*States Parties intending to conclude an agreement referred to in paragraph 3 shall notify the other States Parties through the depositary of this Convention of their intention to conclude the agreement and of the modification or suspension for which it provides.*"

Convention on Mutual Administrative Assistance in Tax Matters (1988)

Article 2 – Taxes covered: "*2. The existing taxes to which the Convention shall apply are listed in Annex A in the categories referred to in paragraph 1.3. The Parties shall notify the Secretary General of the Council of Europe or the Secretary General of OECD (hereinafter referred to as the 'Depositaries') of any change to be made to Annex A as a result of a modification of the list mentioned in paragraph 2. Such change shall take effect on the first day of the month following the expiration of a period of three months after the date of receipt of such notification by the Depositary.*"

Optional Protocol to the Convention on the Rights of the Child on the involvement of children in armed conflict (2000)

Article 3(3): "*2. Each State Party shall deposit a binding declaration upon ratification of or accession to the present Protocol that sets forth the minimum age at which it will permit voluntary recruitment into its national armed forces and a description of the safeguards it has adopted to ensure that such recruitment is not forced or coerced.*"

Article 9(3): "*The Secretary-General, in his capacity as depositary of the Convention and the Protocol, shall inform all States Parties to the Convention and all States that have signed the Convention of each instrument of declaration pursuant to article 3.*"

ii. Communications by the depositary to other parties and relevant stakeholders

67. In accordance with its obligations under public international law, all notifications received by the depositary will be communicated to the other parties to the multilateral instrument.

68. Other relevant stakeholders could be given the possibility to subscribe to an automatic notification system to ensure that they receive the information as soon as it is notified by the depositary. Depositaries to multilateral instruments often set up publicly accessible electronic databases or webpages with all relevant communications from parties (e.g. United Nations Treaty Collection,[17] Council of Europe Treaty Office[18]) and a system of subscriptions to electronic alerts when new documents are added. This would permit all stakeholders to easily access information about the commitments undertaken by each party to the multilateral instrument.

A.3.2 Language versions

69. Given that the multilateral instrument would modify a network of bilateral tax treaties, it is important to consider the question of the official languages of the multilateral instrument. For practical reasons, multilateral instruments are only negotiated and signed in a limited number of languages.

70. Bilateral treaties are usually authenticated in the official language(s) of the pair of parties. Accordingly, the authentic language(s) of bilateral treaties may be different from the language(s) in which the multilateral instrument will be authenticated. It would be possible for official texts in other languages to be established after the signature of the multilateral instrument.

Multilateral Convention for the Avoidance of Double Taxation of Copyright Royalties (1979)

Article 16 – Languages of the convention and notifications: "*1. This Convention shall be signed in a single copy in Arabic, English, French, Russian and Spanish, the five texts being equally authoritative. 2. Official texts shall be established by the Director General of the United Nations Educational, Scientific and Cultural Organization and the Director General of the World Intellectual Property Organization, after consultation with the interested Governments concerned, in the German, Italian and Portuguese languages.*"

71. However, from a practical point of view, it may not be possible to have official texts of the multilateral instrument in all the languages used in bilateral tax treaties. There are many precedents where this difference of languages arises and there are ways to address this. It is important to note that the translation of universal treaties (such as universal human right treaties applied by domestic administrations and tribunals worldwide) to all languages beyond the authentic languages of the multilateral treaty is very common and has created no major difficulties.

72. It would be possible for unofficial translations of the multilateral instrument to be prepared by:

- Individual parties, whose official language is not one of the authentic languages of the multilateral treaty. In most cases, translations will need to be undertaken in any case in order for jurisdictions to complete their domestic requirements to become parties.
- Several parties to the multilateral instrument, which could collaborate in order to agree on a translation in their common language. There are concrete examples of collaboration to prepare an unofficial but co-ordinated translation of a multilateral treaty (e.g. Austria and Germany agreed on a German translation of the MAC).
- The depositary, which could publish unofficial translation of the multilateral instrument (e.g. MAC's unofficial Spanish and Portuguese translations).

73. A mechanism could also be created to address any discrepancies which are identified subsequently between the official languages of the multilateral instrument and/or its unofficial translations.

Conclusion

74. This annex concludes that a multilateral instrument to implement the measures developed in the course of the work on BEPS is feasible and, moreover, would be the most efficient way to modify the existing network of bilateral tax treaties. A multilateral instrument offers an expansive and adaptable toolkit: once the substantive measures have been agreed, all the necessary mechanisms are at our disposal to reflect them as multilateral undertakings while providing defined flexibility in the level of commitment if necessary. The need for transparency and clarity of commitments undertaken by States and their effects on bilateral tax treaties can be addressed through well-tested solutions drawing on treaty law and practice.

75. Once a decision has been taken to work towards a multilateral instrument, the options set out in this paper can be further developed and specified in order to support the negotiation. It will be essential for international tax experts and public international law experts to continue working hand in hand in developing the multilateral instrument in order to draw on the existing treaty law and practice while respecting the specificities of the tax field.

Notes

1. Article 2(1)(a) of the VCLT.

2. Philip Baker (United Kingdom), Théodore Christakis (Greece), Frank Engelen (Netherlands), Concepción Escobar Hernandez (Spain), Mathias Forteau (France), Itai Grinberg (United States), Jan Klabbers (Netherlands), Vaughan Lowe (United Kingdom), Philippe Martin (France), Yoshihiro Masui (Japan), Ekkehart Reimer (Germany), Giorgio Sacerdoti (Italy), Dire Tladi (South Africa).

3. The same analysis applies to regional tax treaties such as the Nordic Convention with respect to Taxes on Income and Capital, the Andean Community Income and Capital Tax Treaty, and the Arab Maghreb Union Income Tax Treaty.

4. Article 30 of the VCLT – Application of successive treaties relating to the same subject-matter: "3. When all the parties to the earlier treaty are parties also to the later treaty but the earlier treaty is not terminated or suspended in operation under article 59, the earlier treaty applies only to the extent that its provisions are compatible with those of the later treaty."

5. The bilateral treaties concluded between the United States (US) and the EU members prior to the entry into force of the EU-US Agreement are still in force.

6. Article 41 of the VCLT – Agreements to modify multilateral treaties between certain of the parties only: "*1. Two or more of the parties to a multilateral treaty may conclude an agreement to modify the treaty as between themselves alone if: (a) the possibility of such a modification is provided for by the treaty; or (b) the modification in question is not prohibited by the treaty and: (i) does not affect the enjoyment by the other parties of their rights under the treaty or the performance of their obligations; (ii) does not relate to a provision, derogation from which is incompatible with the effective execution of the object and purpose of the treaty as a whole. 2. Unless in a case falling under paragraph 1(a) the treaty otherwise provides, the parties in question shall notify the other parties of their intention to conclude the agreement and of the modification to the treaty for which it provides.*"

7. Malcolm N. Shaw, International Law, Cambridge, Sixth Edition, 2008, p. 910: "*The consent of the states parties to the treaty in question is a vital factor, since states may ... be bound only by their consent. Treaties are in this sense contracts between states and if they do not receive the consent of the various states, their provisions will not be binding on them*".

8. Article 34 of the VCLT – General rule regarding third States.

9. Article 35 of the VCLT – Treaties providing for obligations for third States.

10. *Revised Explanatory Report to the Convention on Mutual Administrative Assistance in Tax Matters* as amended by Protocol, www.oecd.org/ctp/exchange-of-tax-information/Explanatory_Report_ENG_%2015_04_2010.pdf.

11. Article 40(4) of the VCLT

12. The International Law Commission devotes two Guidelines in its Guide to Practice on Reservation to Treaties adopted in 2011 (hereafter the "Guide to Practice") to these two mechanisms and provides useful precedents. See doc. A/66/10/Add.1, available at http://legal.un.org/ilc/texts/1_8.htm.

13. Paragraph 1 of the Commentary to Guideline 1.1.6 of the Guide to Practice dedicated to "Reservations formulated by virtue of clauses expressly authorizing the exclusion or the modification of certain provisions of the treaty". According to this Guideline: "*A unilateral statement made by a State or an international organization when that State or organization expresses its consent to be bound by a treaty, in accordance with a clause expressly authorizing the parties or some of them to exclude or to modify the legal effect of certain provisions of the treaty with regard to the party that has made the statement, constitutes a reservation expressly authorized by the treaty.*"

14. Paragraph 1 of the Commentary to Guideline 1.5.3 "Unilateral statements made under a clause providing for options".

15. Article 77(1)(c) of the VCLT – Functions of depositaries.

16. Article 77(1)(e) of the VCLT – Functions of depositaries.

17. United Nations Treaty Collection, https://treaties.un.org/Home.aspx?lang=en.

18. Council of Europe Treaty Office, www.conventions.coe.int/.

Bibliography

G20 (2009), *Declaration on Strengthening the Financial System*, London Summit, 2 April 2009, www.g20ys.org/upload/files/London_2.pdf.

OECD (2014), *Developing a Multilateral Instrument to Modify Bilateral Tax Treaties*, OECD/G20 Base Erosion and Profit Shifting Project, OECD Publishing, Paris, http://dx.doi.org/10.1787/9789264219250-en.

OECD (2013), *Action Plan on Base Erosion and Profit Shifting*, OECD Publishing, http://dx.doi.org/10.1787/9789264202719-en.

Shaw, M. N. (2008) *International Law*, sixth Edition, Cambridge University Press, 2008.

ORGANISATION FOR ECONOMIC CO-OPERATION AND DEVELOPMENT

The OECD is a unique forum where governments work together to address the economic, social and environmental challenges of globalisation. The OECD is also at the forefront of efforts to understand and to help governments respond to new developments and concerns, such as corporate governance, the information economy and the challenges of an ageing population. The Organisation provides a setting where governments can compare policy experiences, seek answers to common problems, identify good practice and work to co-ordinate domestic and international policies.

The OECD member countries are: Australia, Austria, Belgium, Canada, Chile, the Czech Republic, Denmark, Estonia, Finland, France, Germany, Greece, Hungary, Iceland, Ireland, Israel, Italy, Japan, Korea, Luxembourg, Mexico, the Netherlands, New Zealand, Norway, Poland, Portugal, the Slovak Republic, Slovenia, Spain, Sweden, Switzerland, Turkey, the United Kingdom and the United States. The European Union takes part in the work of the OECD.

OECD Publishing disseminates widely the results of the Organisation's statistics gathering and research on economic, social and environmental issues, as well as the conventions, guidelines and standards agreed by its members.

OECD PUBLISHING, 2, rue André-Pascal, 75775 PARIS CEDEX 16
(23 2015 40 1 P) ISBN 978-92-64-24167-1 – 2015-01

www.ingramcontent.com/pod-product-compliance
Lightning Source LLC
LaVergne TN
LVHW080929120826
845149LV00018B/1850

9789264241671